DEDICATION

To all struggling souls who battle adversity every day,

To the hurting hearts of the betrayed and discouraged,

Together we can discover a path of restoration and healing,

Walking by the principles of the word of God.

We will Choose to Win.

◇

B R I A N K I N S E Y

I CHOOSE TO
WIN

HOW TO GET UNSTUCK,
ON TRACK, AND
ENJOY ABUNDANT LIFE

◇

www.BrianKinsey.com

©2019 by Brian Kinsey

©2019 Dust Jacket Press
I Choose to Win, How to Get Unstuck, On Track, and Enjoy Abundant Life / Brian Kinsey

ISBN: 978-1-947671-52-2

Dust Jacket Press
P.O. Box 721243
Oklahoma City, OK 73172
www.dustjacket.com

Ordering information for print editions:
Quantity sales. Special discounts are available on quantity purchases by corporations, associations, and others. For details, check out at www.BrianKinsey.com.

Individual sales. Dust Jacket Press publications are available through most bookstores. They can also be ordered directly from Dust Jacket: Tel: (800) 495-0192; Email: info@dustjacket.com; www.dustjacket.com

Dust Jacket logos are registered trademarks of Dust Jacket Press, Inc.

All Scripture quotations, unless otherwise indicated, are taken from The Holy Bible, King James Version.

Scripture quotations marked (NIV) are taken from The Holy Bible, New International Version®, NIV ®. Copyright ©1973, 1978, 1984, 2011 by Biblica, Inc. Used by permission of Zondervan. All rights reserved worldwide. www.zondervan.com. The "NIV" and "New International Version" are trademarks registered in the United States Patent and Trademark Office by Biblica, Inc.

Scripture quotations marked (TLB) are taken from The Living Bible copyright © 1971. Used by permission of Tyndale House Publishers, Inc., Carol Stream, Illinois 60188. All rights reserved.

Cover & interior design: D.E. West / Dust Jacket Creative Services

Printed in the United States of America

www.BrianKinsey.com

CONTENTS

INTRODUCTION

YOU HAVE A CHOICE TO MAKE

STUCK

Being stuck is a terrible feeling. You could ask any of the sixteen passengers who were stranded on a roller coaster at Fangte Happy World Amusement Park in Wuhu, China. Hoping for a New Year's Eve thrill ride, the passengers boarded a coaster with a corkscrew-like track. As they approached the top of the loop the coaster ground to a halt, possibly due to high winds or the unusually cold weather that day. The screaming tourists were trapped upside-down for half an hour until employees at the massive theme park came to the rescue. No one was seriously injured, but several reported feeling dizzy.[5] That's what happens when you get stuck. You're left helpless, usually in an awkward position, and probably feeling a bit sick. Have you ever felt that way?

It isn't just thrill seekers who sometimes get stuck. It happens to everybody sooner or later. You might get stuck in traffic or stuck in a difficult relationship. You might be stuck with the bill at a restaurant, stuck in unemployment, in credit card debt or bankruptcy. You could be stuck in a dead-end job, an unsatisfying career, a troubled marriage, or a body that has worn out much too soon. Worse, you could be feeling stuck in your past, stuck with

---

5. Lydia Chen, "16 trapped upside-down on roller coaster," *Shanghai Daily* online edition, January 1, 2008, http://www.shanghaidaily.com/news/20080101/343521.

the consequence of the things you've done, or the things someone else has done to you. Grief, divorce, illness, debt, sexual abuse, sexual sin, addiction, disability, obesity, unemployment—there are lots ways to be trapped by seemingly insurmountable circumstances. Maybe you feel stuck right now. Maybe you *are* stuck right now. How does it feel?

Being stuck can produce a variety of emotions, all of them bad. When you get stuck in traffic, you feel frustrated. The same is true when you are stuck in a low-paying job or an unsatisfying marriage. And when you feel trapped, it's natural to look for an object for your frustration or anger or resentment. You may blame others for your condition, or yourself, or even God.

Being stuck can also make you feel helpless, like Ben Carpenter, a twenty-one-year-old man whose electric wheelchair got stuck in the grille of a semi. While Carpenter was crossing a street, the light changed and the truck started forward, catching the wheelchair handles in its grille. The big rig pushed Carpenter and his chair for several miles at speeds up to fifty miles per hour before police officers saw what was happening and signaled the driver to stop.[6] Carpenter, who suffers from muscular dystrophy, later said that he thought he might not make it out of the ordeal alive. Imagine the terror and helplessness of being pushed along the highway, unable to free yourself, unable to call for help. Illness, addiction, and grief can produce that same blend of fear and powerlessness. When you feel trapped by life, you may experience anger, sadness, apathy, dullness, frustration, bitterness, grief, feebleness and hopelessness, perhaps all at the same time. If you are going through a divorce, dealing with an addiction, or

6. David Morgan, "Truck Takes Wheelchair For Wild Ride," CBS News, June 8, 2007, http://www.cbsnews.com/news/truck-takes-wheelchair-for-wild-ride/.

mired beneath a mountain of unpaid bills, you probably know those feelings.

Perhaps the worst result of feeling stuck in life is that it will eventually sap your motivation, causing you to lose hope. You might decide that there's nothing to be done about your circumstance. You may be too embarrassed to ask for help, or you might just be plain exhausted from dealing with your situation. As a result, you may quietly decide to quit looking for solutions. That might be what happened with Safiatou, a nineteen-year-old French woman who got stuck on an elevator for three days. When her father noticed that she was missing, he contacted the building's concierge to say he suspected his daughter was trapped in the lift. But when a repairman checked on the situation, he found nothing amiss. No alarm had been triggered. Two days later a technician returned to complete repairs on the elevator and heard Safiatou's soft cry. She'd been stuck there all along. Nobody knows why she didn't call out for help earlier.[7] Was she embarrassed? Exhausted? Hopeless? Perhaps all three.

Many people who are stuck in adverse circumstances feel they are trapped. They are in painful, frustrating situations because of their own mistakes or the wrongdoing of others, and they simply can't see a way forward. All they see or think about is the grief or the pain or the grinding daily routine that keeps them held in place—sometimes for years. For some, being stuck has become a way of life. No single action seems to be the next right step, so they do nothing. In time, they come to accept their situation as normal. They make peace with their circumstances and by doing so, choose to remain where they are. They choose to be stuck.

---

7. Paul Kevan, "French woman stuck in elevator for 3 days," *Metro*, December 29, 2006, http://metro.co.uk/2006/12/29/french-woman-stuck-in-elevator-for-3-days-3433089/#ixzz1I7c3TgXN.

UNSTUCK

One day Jesus encountered a man who seems to have made the choice to be stuck. We read the story in John chapter 5. The story took place at the pool called Bethesda in ancient Jerusalem. This pool was said to have healing powers. When the waters would stir, or boil up, the first person who stepped into the pool would be healed, so people thought. As a result, sick, lame, and blind folk from all over the region were brought to the five porches surrounding the pool, where they lay around waiting for their next chance at healing. These people were stuck in very bad circumstances and they were desperate for a way out.

Jesus came along one day and engaged one of those people in a conversation, a lame man who had lain by that pool every day for thirty-eight years. *Thirty-eight years!* Talk about being stuck; this man was a poster child for hopelessness. On meeting him, Jesus asked a penetrating question, one that most of us would be too timid to ask of a person who had suffered for so long. Jesus asked him, "Wilt thou be made whole?" (John 5:6). In other words, Jesus was asking, "Do you really want your life to change?" In response, the man rattled off a list of reasons why he had been stuck in that spot for almost four decades. The water wasn't troubled very often. He had difficulty walking. The pool was crowded. Other people always ran ahead of him. Were these legitimate reasons, or was the man merely excusing his inactivity? We can't be sure, and Jesus didn't seem to care one way or the other. He simply said to the man, "Rise, take up thy bed, and walk" (v. 8). The man did exactly that.

Here's the point: You don't have to be stuck! God has the power to free you from the adversity you now face. You may feel trapped, but you are not trapped. Your situation may appear hopeless, but it is not. You may think that your circumstances define your future, but they don't have to. Despite the long time you've been stuck, the problems that never seem to change, the obstacles you just can't overcome, and the many people who seem to be in your way, God has the power to change your life. You can choose to become unstuck. It begins with answering a version of the same question that Jesus asked that lame man by the pool. Do you really want your life to change?

YOUR CHOICE

You have a choice about your future; you really do. When you deny that reality, you surrender your power to choose. In effect, you choose to remain stuck. But when you exercise your freedom of choice, trusting God and accepting his power in your life, you choose victory. You can't change the past—the mistakes you've made, the missed opportunities, or the things others have done to you will always be there. You can, however, take part in changing your future. This begins when you say yes to God's Word and choose to exercise two very potent spiritual choices: hope and faith. No matter what your circumstances are, real change is possible for you. That change will begin when you choose to move forward, when you choose deliverance, when you choose to win.

Making that choice is easier said than done. A number of subtle forces conspire to keep us stuck. One of them is our own pride. We can see that in the humorous example of a man named Xiao Chen, who decided to go for a late-night swim in the Chang Jiang River, only to find himself mired up to the waist in silt. He was stuck in the mud, literally. Although Chen had a cell phone with him, he didn't call for help for some four hours. Imagine being stuck all that time and having a way out but not taking it. In

Chen's case, it was pride that kept him trapped in the mire. He was embarrassed to ask for help. Eventually he called some passing fishermen to his aid, but even then his pride kept him stranded a while longer. The crew that came to Chen's rescue stripped to their underwear before wading into the muck so that they could more easily free him. Incredibly, Chen refused to undo his own trousers so he could be pulled from the mud. He was too embarrassed to ask for help and too proud to accept it when it came. Thankfully, he was eventually liberated.[8]

What about you? Are you willing to do what it takes to get unstuck and claim victory in your life? Are you willing to exercise your power of choice and break free from apathy? Will you rise above your feeling of helplessness and latch onto hope? Will you believe that God can change your life? Will you humble yourself to do whatever God asks of you? If so, you're choosing to win.

THE ROAD AHEAD

The purpose of this book is to give you the understanding and motivation you need to overcome adversity through the power of God. Adversity comes in all shapes and sizes, and the road ahead of you will not be easy. It may take weeks, months, or even years to experience victory, but by making the choice to win you have begun that process. Whether you are suffering from the grief that comes from losing a loved one, the hopelessness that comes from financial stress, or the frustration produced by a toxic relationship, your road to victory begins with the simple decision and elementary principles outlined in this book. You *can* overcome the adversity in your life through the power and grace of God.

---

8. Tom Phillips, "Man stuck in river 'too embarrassed to call for help,'" *Metro*, May 10, 2010, http://metro. co.uk/2010/05/10/man-stuck-in-river-too-embarrassed-to-call-for-help-295469/.

Through these pages, we will look at the way God has dealt with people from the Old Testament times right through today. By examining these great stories, inspiring heroes, and foundational biblical concepts, you will see how God works in our lives through adversity—not just despite it—to bring us to maturity and contentment. And you will find that these principles are not just for Bible heroes like Moses and Joseph and Elisha. They're for everyday people like you and me. There is a way through suffering, a way to rise above adversity and step into God's promise, and you can find it. This book will help you—

- Choose to win by changing your attitude.

- Understand God's work in your life so you can receive his deliverance.

- Move forward in faith, inspired by the great overcomers of the Bible.

Regardless of the negative circumstances you now face, this book will help you move into deliverance, blessing, and peace. *I Choose to Win* contains three sections, each designed to help with a different aspect of your journey.

Part 1 is about *The Choice to Win*. This section will help you choose victory by making four foundational choices that enable you to rise above your challenges. These are four choices:

I choose to believe that change is possible.

I choose to trust God.

I choose to develop a relationship with God.

I choose to obey God.

Make these resolves first in your heart and then put them into action in your life. These are your first steps in overcoming adversity in your life.

Part 2 describes *The Principles of Deliverance*. This section will help you understand how God works in your life—even through the adversity you face—to bring about your deliverance. You will discover key biblical principles for growth by looking at the ways God dealt with his people in the Old Testament. These are the key principles:

> *My present prepares me for God's future.*
>
> *I don't have to wait to be free.*
>
> *I must put myself in a position to win.*
>
> *God works through my weaknesses, not my strengths.*

As you apply this learning to your life, you will grow spiritually despite what you suffer, and you will prepare yourself for victory.

Part 3 paints four *Profiles in Overcoming*. This section will inspire you to move forward in faith based on the examples of great biblical heroes. You'll see that with God, nothing is impossible, and you'll be inspired to persevere in your journey. You will make these discoveries:

> *God has me here for a reason.*
>
> *I gain by giving to others.*
>
> *I grow stronger through hard times.*
>
> *There are better days ahead.*

When you lift your vision to see the possibilities God has for you despite your current circumstances, you will be empowered to move forward into a new life.

Each chapter in this book closes with The Successful Seven, a checklist of action items that will reinforce your choice to win. When you take these steps, you will make great progress toward overcoming the obstacles and adversity you now face. Winning is a revelation and losing is a mindset. When you choose to break free from the losing mindset that keeps you stuck, you are in a position to receive God's help. As you apply the practical life changes described in the book, you will get unstuck and will start making progress. You'll experience the deliverance that God is waiting to reveal for you.

That does not necessarily mean that your external circumstances will change quickly. As you have probably noticed, some faithful people are not healed and not all consequences of sin can be reversed. But while your circumstances *may* change, your life *will* change. When you adopt an attitude of faith, enact the biblical attitudes and principles that lead to deliverance, and joyfully follow the examples of biblical heroes, you will experience the victory, contentment, and peace that has eluded you for so long. And all of that begins with your answer to this simple question:

Do you really want your life to change? If your answer is yes, then you're ready to get unstuck!

◇

PART 1

The Choice to Win

This section will help you choose victory by making four foundational choices that enable you to rise above your challenges. These choices are needed to win:

I choose to believe that change is possible.

I choose to trust God.

I choose to develop a relationship with God.

I choose to obey God.

Make these resolves first in your heart and then put them into action in your life. These are your first steps in overcoming adversity in your life.

◇

◇

1

The Will to Win

See to it that you get your full reward from the Lord.
—2 John 1:8 (TLB)

THE WINNING CHOICE

I choose to believe that change is possible.

WINNING AND LOSING

To understanding winning, you must have a proper definition of losing. Perhaps the best person to provide that definition is Larry Gelwix, one of the winningest coaches in the history of high school athletics. Over a thirty-five-year coaching career, Gelwix led Salt Lake City's Highland High School rugby squad to a 418–10 record.[5] That's an astounding .977 winning percentage. That means that Gelwix's teams lost, on average, only

---

5. "Highland Rugby to Return to Highland High School," Highland Rugby Foundation Web site, October 15, 2012, http://highlandrugby.net/index.php.

one match every three and a half years. It's no wonder he and his coaching philosophy were featured in the 2008 film *Forever Strong*.

What is losing? Larry Gelwix puts it this way: "There is a difference between losing and being beaten. Being beaten means they are better than you. They are faster, stronger, and more talented."[6] To Gelwix, losing means beating yourself by losing sight of what's important and making poor choices. Gelwix taught his players that they must "expect to win" by focusing on the things that matter most and making good decisions in the moment.[7] So while an adversary may defeat you, only you can choose to lose. Australian swimming champion Ian Thorpe put it this way: "For myself, losing is not coming second. It's getting out of the water knowing you could have done better. For myself, I have won every race I've been in."[8]

To lose is to let something slip through your hands. It is to miss an opportunity. When stuck in a poor life situation, you lose by letting victory slip away through lack of faith, apathy, or inaction. And that begins with a losing mindset, the belief that you have no choice, that defeat is inevitable, that there's nothing you can do to reach victory. Therefore, the greatest enemy you face in moving from where you are now to the promise of God is the false idea that you are powerless. The devil wants to deceive you into believing that you must settle for less than what God called you to be. Satan wants you to believe that you can't change, can't overcome, can't win. When you accept that, you will lose. In fact, you have already lost because you have taken yourself out of the contest.

6. Greg McKeown, *Essentialism: The Disciplined Pursuit of Less* (New York: Crown Business, 2014), 216.
7. Paul H. Jenkins and Larry Gelwix, "Living Forever Strong—Re-Uploaded (2010)," Live on Purpose Radio (podcast), April 27, 2010, http://liveonpurposeradio.com/living-forever-strong-re-upload-2010/
8. Piotr J. Kober, *Best Swimming Quotes* (2013), 16.

Revelation is the opposite of deception. Deception is a lie from the devil. Revelation is the truth of God. Deception brings confusion; revelation produces clarity. When you know the truth, you have the ability to relate your current circumstances to the larger story of what God is doing in the world and in your life. It is a deception that "this is as good as it gets" or "the way things are now is how they will always be." That simply isn't true. The revelation of God's Word tells us that God has a purpose for the world and for your life. "For I know the thoughts that I think toward you, saith the LORD, thoughts of peace, and not of evil, to give you an expected end" (Jeremiah 29:11). Though those words were originally spoken to the people of ancient Israel, they are true for you personally as well. God has something good in mind for you, an expected end, or outcome for your life. Nothing in your current circumstances changes that. In fact, God is at work even through the adversity you now face. "And we know that all things work together for good to them that love God, to them who are the called according to his purpose" (Romans 8:28).

When you understand that powerful truth, your circumstances appear in a different light. Rather than seeming to be endless, they point toward a goal. Instead of appearing to be a random series of unfortunate events, your life begins to seem purposeful. When you understand that every event enhances your destiny, you begin to look for signs of God at work, even amid your problems. You stop asking "What's next?" with a spirit of fear and trepidation and start asking "What's next?" with an air of excitement. A person living in deception will be hopeless, doubtful, and stuck. A person that has revelation gains the ability to look at everything that has transpired in his or her life and see that it has a higher purpose and will eventually turn out to be good.

In this chapter, you will learn about the freedom God has given you to choose between death and life. You will be empowered to make the choice to pursue life, blessing, peace, and promise. That begins with your choice to believe that your decisions determine your destiny.

GOD DESIRES VICTORY

Losing is a learned behavior so one challenge we face in overcoming adversity is to get beyond the faulty theology that teaches us to be negative, depressive, and oppressive. The starting point is to understand this truth from the Word: God is a God of victory, and He wants you to win.

A view of God and the Christian life that has become popular holds that the point of life is to suffer. According to this view, God is a kindly helper who gives us cheer and comfort but is too weak to do anything about our circumstances. This way of thinking pictures God as a well-meaning, hand-wringing worrier, not a powerful savior. Not surprisingly, this way of thinking leads to the idea that suffering is both inevitable and interminable. "Life is short and then you die" might be the motto of Christians who hold this view. They see the point of human existence as to endure the awful world in which we are trapped. We must hunker down and ride out the storm until Jesus comes back to take us to Heaven. To them, victory is reserved entirely for the other side of eternity. Only in heaven can we have freedom, joy, health, provision, and peace. For now, we wait.

The problem with that view is that it is incomplete and therefore unbiblical. It is true that the Holy Ghost is our Comforter. We have the Spirit of God to bring us hope and encouragement and to guide us in prayer, but the Comforter is also our Teacher.

Jesus said, "The Comforter, which is the Holy Ghost, whom the Father will send in my name, he shall teach you all things, and bring all things to your remembrance, whatsoever I have said unto you" (John 14:26). Revealing truth is a primary work of the Spirit. The Comforter comes not merely to help us endure suffering but also to arm us with revelation so that we can gain a heavenly perspective. And what is that heavenly perspective? It is that God is an overcomer and desires that we should be overcomers too.

God wants to overwhelm our circumstances with truth and overcome our helplessness with hope. He wants victory for himself, for his people, and for you. The psalmist writes, "O clap your hands, all ye people; shout unto God with the voice of triumph" (Psalm 47:1). God invites his people to lift up a song of victory. "But what about my problems?" you might wonder. "How can I have an attitude of victory in the midst of adversity?" It's a fair question. It is hard to sing the songs of Zion in a "strange land," meaning that it's hard to see victory when you're surrounded by defeat (see Psalm 137:4). But remember that the great saints of the Bible also faced adversity and they praised God anyway. Even when David was on the run from Saul and living in the wilderness to keep from being put to death, he was able to write these words: "I sought the LORD, and he heard me, and delivered me from all my fears" (Psalm 34:4) and "Be of good courage, and he shall strengthen your heart, all ye that hope in the LORD" (Psalm 31:24).

Having a revelation of truth allows you to see beyond the horizon. It allows you to look past the way things are at the moment to see how they will be through the power of God. David knew that God would come to his rescue regardless of how bad the situation was. As a result, David was able to praise God *dur-*

ing his adversity. That's the attitude of empowerment that results from revelation.

God is in control from beginning to end. He started at the finish line and went back to the starting line. Christ was crucified before the beginning of time. God is the author and finisher of our faith. He is the producer and the director, and he wrote the screenplay for your life. The script belongs to him, and the ending has already been written. When you understand your destiny, you will realize that you cannot lose.

Remember the definition of losing. It is letting victory slip through your fingers by your own choices. In this game of life, each of us has a rival. Your greatest rival is not any other person, nor even the devil himself. Your greatest rival is you. The apostle Paul wrote on this very subject, and I like the way his words are rendered in *The Message*.

> *You've all been to the stadium and seen the athlete's race. Everyone runs; one wins. Run to win. All good athletes train hard. They do it for a gold medal that tarnishes and fades. You're after one that's gold eternally. I don't know about you, but I'm running hard for the finish line. I'm giving it everything I've got. No sloppy living for me! I'm staying alert and in top condition. I'm not going to get caught napping, telling everyone else all about it and then missing out myself. (1 Corinthians 9:24–27)*

Many Christians have become far too accustomed to losing. When we lose a marriage, or a soul from the kingdom, or lose a job or an important opportunity, we think, *Oh well, that's just the way it goes.* No, it isn't! It is time to stop accepting defeat, to stop being stuck in place, to stop believing that your job in life is to suffer patiently and never gain victory. God is an overcoming God and he empowers his people to be overcomers too. Do not allow the deception of the devil to convince you otherwise. Do not allow Satan to interrupt your future or destroy your destiny. God has an inheritance prepared for you. Do not take yourself out of the race by deciding that you are licked already. Run so as to get the prize. "See to it that you get your full reward from the Lord" (2 John 1:8 TLB).

CHOOSING EMPOWERMENT

Good decisions are easier to make than they are to enact. You may have experienced that when attempting a New Year's resolution. You make a choice or enter into a commitment with the best intentions only to find yourself right back where you started after just a few weeks, maybe just a few days. That's typical. While about 41 percent of people make New Year's resolutions, most don't keep them. Fewer than half of those who make resolutions will stick with them longer than six months, and only about 9 percent are successful in achieving their goal.[9] Why is that?

One reason is that most people make choices based on *emotion* but fail to support those decisions with *action.* Passion can take you only so far. Once you have gotten up from the altar of prayer or returned to school, or in this case, finished the book, the resolve wears off. Your overcoming attitude evaporates amid the noise and confusion of everyday life. To be successful over the long term, you must support your decision with sturdy practices that reinforce your choice. Your attitude needs a plan.

---

9. Statistic Brain Research Institute, "New Years Resolution Statistics," Statistic Brain Web site, January 1, 2017, http://www.statisticbrain.com/new-years-resolution-statistics/.

Here are three solid actions that will support your choice to be an overcomer. Do these things, and you will not only feel empowered but also be empowered to overcome adversity and claim the promise God has for you.

1. DO EVERYTHING ON PURPOSE

People who make good small decisions make good large decisions. When you do the next right thing in each moment, you will have no trouble accomplishing the great big thing that God has in mind for you. Likewise, if you blow all the small choices, you'll never make progress toward your big goal. You must support your decision to overcome by doing everything on purpose, making each choice align with your overall goal to be an overcomer.

The apostle Paul was a sports fan, or at least he understood the strong parallel between athletic competition and the Christian life. Both are goal-oriented, and both require a strong sense of purpose. In one of his many sports analogies, Paul writes, "Therefore I do not run like someone running aimlessly; I do not fight like a boxer beating the air" (1 Corinthians 9:26 NIV). Imagine the contrast between a marathon runner and a shadow boxer. The marathon runner has a long race ahead, and he must remain focused. You may have seen those distance athletes, their eyes fixed on the horizon with steely resolve written on their faces. They have a single focus, and that focus affects every choice they make from what to do in their spare time, to when they get up in the morning, and even what foods they eat. Every choice aligns with their goal and they will not be distracted from it.

A shadow boxer doesn't have a focus. Though he is moving constantly, taking jabs and throwing roundhouses, there's no opponent in front of him. There's no goal, no adversary to overcome.

He's just waving his arms for practice. He's beating the air but accomplishing nothing.

Paul's point is that you must live your life on purpose, arranging every choice you make to advance your goal. He goes on to say, "I strike a blow to my body and make it my slave so that after I have preached to others, I myself will not be disqualified for the prize" (1 Corinthians 9:27 NIV). Paul knew that without a strong sense of purpose, victory could easily slip through his fingers, so he aligned every action with his overall goal to be faithful to Christ.

You too must have a purpose for your life, and to achieve it you must align every decision and action with that goal. Too many people make the bold choice to follow Christ, to overcome adversity, and to claim the promise he has for them, only to return to life as usual. They continue living life just as they always have, never working out their decision in the arena of everyday life. They decide to improve their marriage but fall back into the same selfishness and poor communication that led to a breakdown in the first place. They make the choice to improve their health but quickly resume the same habit of eating junk food. If you are going to make positive change in your life, you must examine every choice you make in the light of your overall goal. Regarding each decision, large or small, ask, "Does this help me win today?"

Remember also that you will not be making these choices in a vacuum. You have an enemy, the devil, who wants nothing more than to distract you from your purpose. Now that you have made the choice to move forward, the devil will try to convince you there's no point—that your life does not have a purpose and so your choices are meaningless. "So what?" he'll say, causing you to question whether anything you do really matters. Sometimes he'll draft other people into his service, prompting them to say discouraging things to you or about you.

That's what happened to the young boy David when he attempted to live out his purpose. His own brother tried to discourage him. David was an overcomer, and he had an attitude of empowerment. So when he heard about the giant Goliath, he saw it as an opportunity, not a problem. But his brother Eliab was a negative thinker, stuck in the idea that nobody could do anything to defeat the giant. "And Eliab's anger was kindled against David, and he said, Why camest thou down hither? and with whom hast thou left those few sheep in the wilderness? I know thy pride, and the naughtiness of thine heart; for thou art come down that thou mightest see the battle. And David said, What have I now done? Is there not a cause? And he turned from him toward another, and spake after the same manner: and the people answered him again after the former manner" (1 Samuel 17:28–30).

It's hard to remain focused when other people, especially those closest to you, belittle your plans or criticize what you're doing. But David refused to be pulled off purpose by the negative attitudes of those around him. David knew that losers run away from their problems because they feel inadequate or afraid, but winners run to their problems because they know that facing the giant brings you one step closer to victory. That's the attitude of empowerment in action.

Are you determined to win? Are you ready to claim the promise that God has for you in your marriage, your finances, your health, your ministry? That's wonderful. Now what is the next thing you must do to reach that goal? How will your choices today help or hurt you in achieving your purpose? Right now, what is the most important thing you can do to win? Examine everything you do in light of your goal and refuse to be pulled off purpose by trivial actions, laziness, or negative people. Do everything on purpose. Otherwise you will fall into the trap the apostle Paul warned about, waving your arms in a flurry of activity but accomplishing nothing.

2. SURROUND YOURSELF WITH OVERCOMERS

The attitude of empowerment is contagious. When you choose to win and organize your life around that goal, others will be attracted to your strong sense of resolve. And that's important because there is no greater influence upon you than the company you keep. When you surround yourself with overcomers, those who have chosen to base their lives on hope and faith, you place yourself in a position to win. The opposite is also true. When you surround yourself with negative thinkers, folk who are stuck in the mud of cynicism, despair, or hopelessness, you'll have a difficult time keeping your focus. The Proverbs tell us, "Make no friendship with an angry man; and with a furious man thou shalt not go: Lest thou learn his ways, and get a snare to thy soul" (Proverbs 22:24–25). Surround yourself with winners, not whiners.

In particular, it is important to have a mentor or guide who has advanced further in life and faith than you have. You need a coach. A coach is part encourager, part accountability partner, part mentor, and part drill sergeant. A good coach will be a friend who sticks closer to you than a brother, someone who will say, "You can!" when you're convinced you can't. A coach is someone with the experience, wisdom, and maturity to tell you "Stop!" when you're on the verge of wandering from your purpose. A person who lives by preference and not principle easily gets off track. A coach holds you to your principles.

You also need like-minded friends who are intent on overcoming adversity and making positive change in their lives. A coach or mentor is someone who has advanced beyond you. You also need teammates who walk along with you in the everyday moments of life. These are the coworkers who will encourage you to reach your performance goals, the fellow dieters who will celebrate your weight loss victories, the students who are trying to remain faithful in a secular environment just as you are. Surround yourself with people who live by the same convictions you do, and they will support your attitude of empowerment.

This matters a great deal because Scripture warns that even in the church there will be those who live by preference rather than principle. Paul writes, "But mark this: There will be terrible times in the last days. People will be lovers of themselves, lovers of money, boastful, proud, abusive, disobedient to their parents, ungrateful, unholy, without love, unforgiving, slanderous, without self-control, brutal, not lovers of the good, treacherous, rash, conceited, lovers of pleasure rather than lovers of God—having a form of godliness but denying its power. Have nothing to do with such people" (2 Timothy 3:1–5 NIV).

Let's read that last statement again: *"Have nothing to do with such people."* Does that sound harsh? It isn't. With eternity at stake, you cannot afford to allow people with a losing mindset into your inner circle. This doesn't mean that you should not witness to or influence those who need help and hope. It simply means that you must protect your mind and heart by not allowing those who are living for no purpose to get too close to you. Choose your friends and associates wisely. Surround yourself with overcomers and they will strengthen your attitude and your resolve.

3. PRACTICE SELF-CONTROL

If you are a parent or have observed small children, then you know there is a critical moment in the development of any child. It is the moment when that child learns the word *no*. Sometimes this moment is comical, as when a one-year-old wants to play with the remote control. When told no, the happy toddler breaks into crocodile tears with exaggerated wailing. Even in their mock distress, kids can be hilariously endearing. Yet that moment is important because if a child cannot learn to accept "no" in unimportant things, he or she will be unable to say no in more weighty matters later on. How many lives have been ruined because of the inability to place self-imposed limits on behavior?

If you are to succeed in overcoming the adversity you now face, you must learn to say no to yourself. You must learn the discipline of self-control. People without self-control are dangerous to themselves and others. They act on every impulse that enters their heads. They overindulge their bodily appetites, spend too much money, say things without thinking, and follow preference over principle at every opportunity. Without self-control, you cannot hope to align your daily choices with your overall purpose. You will become a slave to whatever urge seems strongest at the moment. With self-control, you will be able to say no to your selfish desires and yes to the habits, attitudes, and actions that will help you reach your goal.

Self-control is a practice, meaning that it's something you must do continually until it becomes a habit. To jump-start your self-control, identify the areas of your life where you are most easily distracted or pulled into sin. What are the things you generally wind up regretting? Once you know where those pressure points are, you can strengthen your self-control through these simple strategies.

Make Yourself Accountable. Tell someone you trust about your struggle. Ask them to advise you and hold you to account. Knowing that someone is going to ask you about your choices or behavior provides a strong motivation to do what's right.

Remind Yourself of Your Decision. Daily restate your decision to overcome. Throughout the day, ask yourself, "How does this thought or action help me reach my goals?" Simply asking the question will strengthen your ability to choose right.

Stay Away from Trouble. You already know what your pressure points are. Now list the people, places, and situations that make it more difficult for you to be self-disciplined. If you cannot maintain a positive attitude around certain friends, make different friends. If you tend to make poor choices when you are hungry, angry, lonely, or tired, be careful not to push the limits of your body and mind. Stay rested and healthy. Chances are good that you already know the *who, where,* and *when* that pull you off track. Avoid them.

Build on Victory. Self-control begins with one simple decision to say no to an urge or appetite. That's difficult to do in the moment because our emotions can be overwhelming. But it does get easier with practice. Build on each small victory, and your self-control muscle will become stronger and stronger. You can overcome!

Pray. You have a source of strength available to you that is far stronger than your own willpower. You have access to the power of God through prayer. When your strength is exhausted, his has not yet begun. When you can't, he can. Pray daily for the fruit of self-control and pray immediately when you face the temptation to give in to selfish desires.

If you want to be a winner, you must practice self-control. Without self-control, you will never win. With it, you cannot lose.

I CHOOSE TO WIN

Your decision determines your destiny. If you choose to believe that no positive change is possible, then none will occur. If you accept your current circumstances as permanent, they will become so. If you decide to lose, your destiny is decided.

However, the converse is also true. If you decide to win, your destiny is decided in the opposite direction. If you choose to believe that God is an overcomer and he wants victory for you, you will win. If you refuse to accept the idea that your circumstances are permanent, they will change. There is tremendous power in your choice, a power that God has placed in your hands.

Winning, however, is not a quick or easy objective. It can take a bit of time, and it is likely to involve a number of setbacks. To maintain an attitude of empowerment, you must prepare yourself for the long haul. That's why it's critical to support your decision with positive actions. You cannot afford to become discouraged when obstacles come your way.

If you enjoy football, you may know something about the life and career of John Elway, who led the Denver Broncos to back-to-back Super Bowl victories following the 1997 and 1998 seasons. During his sixteen years in pro football, Elway amassed dozens of records and honors, including being selected for the Pro Bowl nine times. He was elected to the Pro Football Hall of Fame in 2004.

Yet many are less familiar with these facts about the legendary athlete. Though he was a highly touted newcomer when he entered the league in 1983, John Elway performed so poorly in his first professional game that he had to be relieved by a veteran backup quarterback. Halfway through his first season, Elway was benched. And while he is best known for winning consecutive Super Bowls in the 1990s, a younger John Elway lost the Super Bowl three times, including a 55–10 defeat by the San Francisco 49ers, the worst shellacking in Super Bowl history.

Yet a winner doesn't lose focus, and young Elway kept his eye on the prize. In his final NFL appearance, he was named the most-valuable player of Super Bowl XXXIII and, at age thirty-eight, became the oldest player ever to score a touchdown in the NFL's championship game.

Over the coming days, you are certain to experience some knockdowns. Making the choice to overcome will not place you in the winner's circle overnight. There will be difficult days and hard battles ahead. But a setback is not a loss. Being knocked down does not determine your destiny; only your decision to stay down can seal your fate. Will you prevail? Will you overcome the difficulties you now face in life? Will your circumstances change? One thing is for sure: nothing will change until you believe it can.

In Revelation 2:7, we read, "He that hath an ear, let him hear what the Spirit saith unto the churches; To him that overcometh will I give to eat of the tree of life, which is in the midst of the paradise of God." This is the reward in store for those who choose to win. It's a goal worth fighting for. That word *overcome* means victory. And we know that in ancient Greek mythology, the winged goddess of victory was called Nike. It's time to lace up your Nikes.

You have chosen to win, and you must now make that choice a reality.

And you must persevere in that decision. You can't be double-minded and be a winner. Though the decision to overcome is an emotional one, it cannot be made on emotion alone. You must choose to win with your whole mind. As James says, "But let him ask in faith, nothing wavering. For he that wavereth is like a wave of the sea driven with the wind and tossed. For let not that man think that he shall receive any thing of the Lord. A double minded man is unstable in all his ways" (James 1:6–8). Make this choice, then support it with the positive actions that reinforce your will to overcome. That will help you finish strong. The devil is not worried about people who start out to do good because most of them will not finish. But when you back your decision with true resolve, you become a threat to Satan's kingdom.

Jesus said, "It is finished" (John 19:30). Paul wrote, "I have finished my course" (2 Timothy 4:7). The writer of Hebrews said that Jesus is "the author and finisher of our faith" (Hebrews 12:2). You have made the decision to win. You have made the choice to believe that better things are possible, that God has a promise in store for you, that you will overcome. Don't stop short. Fight the good fight. Finish the race. See to it that you get your full reward from the Lord.

THE SUCCESSFUL SEVEN

- Write down your goal, the obstacle or adversity over which you are seeking victory.

- List several daily actions that will support your goal.

- Name one person who could help you succeed and make an appointment to speak with that person about becoming your coach.

- Name three people you want to spend more time with because of their positive attitude.

- List the places, people, and situations you must avoid in order to maintain an attitude of empowerment.

- Pray for the strength to say no to your preferences and live by your principles.

- Memorize 2 John 1:8 and 1 Corinthians 9:26.

◇

2
Adversity to Advantage

*Offer unto God thanksgiving; and pay thy vows unto
the most High: And call upon me in the day of trouble:
I will deliver thee, and thou shalt glorify me.*
—Psalm 50:14–15

THE WINNING CHOICE

I choose to trust God.

YOUR FIRST CALL

When you're in trouble, the best thing to do is call for help. So it's good when you have the phone number of someone who can actually solve your problem. It's even better when that person is someone you trust. For example, if you knew for sure that your father could get you out of a jam, you'd probably relax a little bit and you'd certainly make that call. That's what Mark Ashton-Smith did, but the circumstances were a bit unusual. When Ashton-Smith, who was at the time a thirty-three-year-old lecturer in psychology at University of Cambridge, got into a pickle, it was something far worse than a flat tire or an unexpected bill for home repair. He had capsized while kayaking in rough seas just off the coast of England. And his father, Alan Pimm-Smith, wasn't just around the corner. He was some 3,500 miles away in the United Arab Emirates on an assignment to train British troops.

When the tiny craft overturned, dumping Ashton-Smith into frigid waters near the Isle of Wight, he did everything you might think to do in those circumstances. He tried to climb back aboard. He attempted to maneuver himself to shore. He even sounded a foghorn to alert any passing ships. Nothing worked. Finally, he reached into the toe of his kayak and fished out a cell phone. After struggling to pry open the watertight container with icy fingers, Smith placed two calls: one to his sister in Cambridge, a four-and-a-half-hour drive away, and the other to his father in Dubai. Both alerted the coastguard station at Solent, less than a mile from the stranded kayaker's location. He was rescued within the hour.[10] It's great to have a dad you can count on.

You too have a Father who is a great help in times of need. The psalmist tells us, "God is our refuge and strength, a very present help in trouble" (Psalm 46:1). When you face adversity of any kind, you have a direct line to the One who can provide deliverance. It does not matter how grave the situation may be or how distant from the Lord you may feel. He has given you this promise: "Call upon me in the day of trouble: I will deliver thee"

---

10. "Capsized canoeist calls Dubai for help," BBC News, September 10, 2001, http://kochhars.com/2/hi/uk_news/1535936.stm.

(Psalm 50:15). When you have trouble to overcome, your first resort should be to call on God.

That's important to know because although you have already chosen to believe that your decision decides your destiny, you may still feel stuck. You may *be* stuck. There are things in your life that you cannot change on your own. Choosing to move forward in faith does not mean that all your problems will have disappeared overnight. You may face difficulty in marriage, and you have no doubt learned that you cannot make another person change or love you. You're changing, but your marriage may still be the same. You may face financial difficulties. If so you have likely figured out that you cannot manufacture money. Your decision has made a change in you, but you still face a real problem. You need help. So the next decision you must make is to trust God. You must believe that no matter how immovable the obstacles may seem, God has the power to deliver you. When you trust God, you will call out to him. Without that trust, you will probably never make that call.

In this chapter, you will learn about the trust relationship you must develop with God in order to experience deliverance. You will see that relationship in the simple formula expressed in Psalm 50:15. That formula begins with calling upon God for help. "Call upon me in the day of trouble." In order to call upon God, you must have complete faith in him. You must trust him enough to call out for help.

WHY WE GO IT ALONE

Surprisingly, calling on God for help is not the first thought that comes to most people's minds when facing adversity. Like the capsized kayaker who first tried to rescue himself, we often exhaust our own resources, and ourselves, before we "give in" and reach out to God. Perhaps you've noticed that tendency in yourself. When you feel unwell, you may first try to ignore your symptoms. Then you try a home remedy or two. If the discomfort becomes too intense, you ask a friend for advice. Doubled over in pain, you may eventually visit the doctor. Only when the doctor says "I've got some bad news" do you call on your heavenly Father in prayer. Why are we so reluctant to call on God for the help we know he can provide? There may be several reasons.

We Think We Must Be Strong. Some of us were raised with the attitude that we should be self-reliant and solve our own problems. We don't ask for God's help because we mistakenly believe that we shouldn't need it. We reason that if we ask for help, it shows that we are not as strong or spiritual or mature as we should be. But everyone needs help from the Lord. We are all fallible creatures. We have needs, and God wants us to come to him with those needs. "Call upon me in the day of trouble," God tells us (Psalm 50:15).

We Wonder If We Can Trust God. A second reason some people hesitate to reach out to God is that they don't see him as completely trustworthy. "If God were really all that good," they think, "I wouldn't be experiencing these problems to begin with." You may wonder about that, or other questions like these:

- If God is so good, why does he allow people to suffer?

- If God is in control of everything, then isn't he the one causing my pain?

- Doesn't the fact that there is suffering in the world prove that God is not strong enough to do anything about it?

Those questions appear to be compelling on the surface, but let's think about them a little deeper. In regard to the first question, "If God is so good, why does he allow people to suffer?" let's think of it this way. There are lots of reasons why a loving father might allow his children to experience problems. A good parent will sometimes let children risk pain, frustration, and failure in order to grow. Good parents don't step in too quickly. Learning can be a painful process. And there may be many reasons God allows the suffering in the world or in our lives. To teach us to grow and to prompt us to show love to one another are just two possible reasons. In the end, we selfish human beings would have a hard time accusing God of being unfair. He is far greater, wiser, and kinder than we are. We don't always understand what he does or why.

As to the second question, "If God is in control of everything, then isn't he the one causing my pain?" let's use the analogy of parenting again. A mom who chooses to let her daughter play softball understands that there is some risk of injury. People get hurt playing sports all the time. So when the girl falls and breaks an arm, is the mother responsible? Yes, in the sense that parents are always responsible for the things their children do. But does that mean the mom *wanted* her daughter to experience pain? Of course not. Allowing suffering and inflicting it are two different things. God allows adversity in our lives and even uses it to accomplish a purpose, but he desires only good for us.

Regarding the third question, "Doesn't the fact that there is suffering in the world prove that God is not strong enough to do anything about it?" does that reasoning hold true? The fact that God *could* intervene to stop suffering does not mean that he *must* do so. God has the power of choice. He can choose to act or choose not to act. Because God is silent sometimes does not mean he cannot speak. And because he refrains from intervening in a situation doesn't mean that he cannot do so—or that he will not at some point. Remember the words of the apostle Peter, "But, beloved, be not ignorant of this one thing, that one day is with the Lord as a thousand years, and a thousand years as one day. The Lord is not slack concerning his promise, as some men count slackness; but is longsuffering to us-ward, not willing that any should perish, but that all should come to repentance" (2 Peter 3:8–9). God does not operate on our timetable or according to our goals, but that doesn't mean he does not care about what you are experiencing right now. God is good, and you *can* trust him.

We're Too Proud. A third reason some people hesitate to call on God is that they are simply too prideful to admit that they need help. They fear looking needy or, worse yet, actually being dependent on God or others. That kind of pride has a simple name: sin. It is the pride that drove Adam and Eve into the original sin in the Garden of Eden. They wanted to be independent of God, so they believed the devil's lie and ate the fruit that they thought would make them "as gods" (Genesis 3:5). We're still dealing with the fallout from that prideful act today.

God wants us to call on him when we are in need precisely because we *do* depend on him. We are weak, but he is strong. We are limited, and he is limitless. There's no point in pretending otherwise.

CALLING ON GOD

Let's look closer at the first portion of Psalm 50:15, the command to call upon God for help. Why does God insist on this? If God is all-powerful, he must certainly know what our needs are.

Why does he stipulate that we must reach out for help before he will provide it? There are a number of good reasons for this. Let's start with the most basic one. In the very act of calling on God for help, we are giving him glory.

CALLING ON GOD BRINGS HIM GLORY

One reason God asks us to call out to him when we're in need is that it brings him glory. God is all-knowing, so he already knows what you need. Jesus said as much in his Sermon on the Mount. When it comes to the daily needs we all have, Jesus said, "…for your heavenly Father knoweth that ye have need of all these things" (Matthew 6:32). We don't call out to God to inform him of our troubles; we call out to show our dependence on him. Calling out to God is an act of worship.

Observe a small child interacting with a parent and you will quickly notice that kids call out to their parents in two situations—or in two ways. The first is for something they want. They want to be picked up. They want attention. They want a toy or a cracker. Parents can easily discern when their child's cry is based on want. It has a demanding tone. Though not yet able to speak, the child is saying, "I want!" If we're honest, we'll admit that many of our prayers are "I want!" prayers.

The second reason a child cries out to a parent is because of need. The child may be hurt or afraid and desperately needs help and reassurance. Parents find it easy to distinguish this kind of cry from the other. An "I need you!" cry comes from the heart. It voices real emotion. This is the kind of cry to which parents respond.

When we cry out to God from the depths of our need, our prayers have a different quality. They show that we are at the end of our rope, and we believe God is our only solution. There is a great difference between asking for a favor and crying out in distress. The first type of cry is all about us. The second is all about God. It is a truthful recognition of who God is. Calling on God in the time of trouble brings glory to him in itself. This is the kind of cry that prompts God's response.

CALLING ON GOD RISES FROM A RELATIONSHIP

As we're looking at Psalm 50, it's important to pull back a bit and see the context in which these words were written. This offer to call on God when in trouble is sandwiched between two other statements that pinpoint its meaning. The first one comes in verse 7. There God says, "Hear, O my people, and I will speak; O Israel, and I will testify against thee: I am God, even thy God. I will not reprove thee for thy sacrifices or thy burnt offerings, to have been continually before me."

What we discover there is that God had a legitimate complaint about his people. He had no problem with their visible religion, the outward worship and their ceremonies. They were doing the right things—making the proper sacrifices as an act of worship. But God did have a problem with their heart. He knew that their heart was not in the things they were doing. They were just going through the motions. Ritual has very little meaning to God. He doesn't understand the language of pomp and show. God wants to hear an honest cry from the heart.

Trouble has a way of adding virtue to our prayers and revealing the true nature of our relationship with God. It reveals the depth of our spirituality. It adds intensity. Too often, we're like the toy spinning tops that children use for play. They don't spin unless they are whipped. When we are laid low by adversity, the true nature of our relationship with God is revealed. That's why God begins his offer of deliverance in verse 14 with these words, "Offer unto God thanksgiving; and pay thy vows unto the most High." When we are in tune with God, offering him daily praise and thanks from a sincere heart, we're in a position to call on him with integrity.

The second verse that adds context to this offer of deliverance is verse 16 of Psalm 50. There we read, "But unto the wicked God saith, What hast thou to do to declare my statutes, or that thou shouldest take my covenant in thy mouth?" He later adds, "Now consider this, ye that forget God, lest I tear you in pieces, and there be none to deliver" (verse 22). Clearly, this offer of deliverance is for those who are in a relationship with God. Our sincere cry to God, from the heart and accompanied by praise, is a demonstration of our relationship with him.

If you are in a relationship with God, calling on him for help will be your first resort. If you are not walking with the Lord, calling on him to solve a problem won't do any good. Our cry for help must rise from a relationship with the Lord. If you are not walking closely with God, take the psalmist's advice and "Offer unto God thanksgiving; and pay thy vows unto the most High" (verse 14). Turn to him now with your whole heart. Then you'll be in a position to ask for help when you need it most.

CALLING ON GOD SHOWS THAT WE TRUST HIM

Calling on God is an expression of faith. It shows that we trust him. We have confidence that he can do what he has promised. The very act of asking for help is an expression of our faith. If God can find even a trace of faith anywhere in you, he will deliver you.

When we work overtime to solve our problems without God, we're really displaying the opposite of faith. We're acting on pride, the belief that we don't need God. That's what leads us to adopt a religion that's mostly ritual and prayers that are mostly for show. We're doing what we do to bring attention to ourselves, not to bring glory to God or to sincerely admit our dependence on him. We see that trust displayed over and over in the prayers of the saints. Psalm 27 is a fine example. The psalmist writes: "The LORD is my light and my salvation; whom shall I fear? the LORD is the strength of my life; of whom shall I be afraid? When the wicked, even mine enemies and my foes, came upon me to eat up my flesh, they stumbled and fell. Though an host should encamp against me, my heart shall not fear: though war should rise against me, in this will I be confident" (Psalm 27:1–3). That's the kind of trust that glorifies God and shows our utter confidence in him. God responds to that call for help.

There's a story often told about Alexander the Great that demonstrates the kind of complete confidence that God desires in us. We ought to trust God as implicitly as Alexander trusted his friend, who was also his physician. The physician had mixed a medicine for Alexander, who was sick, and left the potion by Alexander's bed for him to drink. Just before Alexander drank it, a letter was delivered to him in which he was warned that his physician had been bribed to poison him. Alexander read the letter, then summoned the physician into his presence. When he came in, Alexander picked up the cup of medicine, drank it, then handed his friend the letter.[11] That's a high degree of trust, and that's exactly what God is looking for in us.

11. C. H. Spurgeon, "Prayer to God in Trouble an Acceptable Sacrifice," *The Metropolitan Tabernacle Pulpit: Sermons Preached and Revised by C. H. Spurgeon, During the Year 1879*, Vol. XXV (London: Passmore & Alabaster, 1880), 654–655.

When we call out to God from a sincere heart, we acknowledge our utter dependence on him. But we don't call out to God because there is no alternative. God is not our last resort. We call out to God because we have absolute confidence that he will come to our aid. Hide nothing from God. Reserve nothing. Tell him everything that's in your heart, and then trust him about it all. When you have placed your burden before the Lord, leave it with him. Say to yourself, "My soul, wait thou only upon God; for my expectation is from him. He only is my rock and my salvation: he is my defence; I shall not be moved" (Psalm 62:5–6).

I WILL DELIVER

The first part of Psalm 50:15 is our invitation to call out to God when we're in trouble. This is our response: to exercise our faith in the context of a relationship with the father and to cry out for help. When we do that, it demonstrates our complete confidence in him. Now let's look at the second part of this formula, which is God's response. Let's notice the two parts of this statement: "I will deliver thee, and thou shalt glorify me." When we call out to God, he will deliver us, but that's not all. That deliverance will prompt a response in us. We'll be changed by what God does for us.

GOD WILL DELIVER YOU

God's invitation is accompanied by a promise. When we call out to him, he *will* deliver us. God doesn't say, "I will think about you," or, "I will feel sorry for you." He doesn't say, "I will provide a few resources that might be helpful to you." He says, "I will deliver you." That's a promise of solid, substantial help. This promise is similar to the statement Moses made to the Israelites when they were being pursued by the Egyptian army after leaving Egypt. You can read that story in Exodus 14.

The people were trapped up against the Red Sea with the Egyptians bearing down on them. Scripture records, "And when Pharaoh drew nigh, the children of Israel lifted up their eyes, and, behold, the Egyptians marched after them; and they were sore afraid: and the children of Israel cried out unto the LORD" (Exodus 14:10). The Israelites were in desperate need, and they did exactly what God invites us to do: they cried out to God for help. Now listen to what Moses said to them, "Fear ye not, stand still, and see the salvation of the LORD, which he will shew to you to day: for the Egyptians whom ye have seen to day, ye shall see them again no more for ever. The LORD shall fight for you, and ye shall hold your peace" (Exodus 14:13–14).

When you call out to God amid adversity, you can expect his response. You can stand like Noah amid the flood, having perfect confidence that God's salvation is secure. You will be like the three young men, Shadrach, Meshach, and Abednego, who stood tall in the fiery furnace and came out unharmed. You will go through the trouble triumphantly because you will have God's sustaining grace. And you know that your life has a purpose. Your adversity has "an expected end" (Jeremiah 29:11). Remember that Joseph emerged from prison to rule a nation. David may have hidden in caves for a while, but he later sat upon a throne. Daniel had to go into the lion's den, but he was taken from there to a position of honor. We can expect God's deliverance because we know that he has greater things in mind for us.

Notice also that this promised deliverance is personal. God says, "I will deliver thee." He himself will undertake on our behalf. When you know *who* will deliver you, you can be content not knowing the *how* or the *when*. As the apostle Paul put it, "If God be for us, who can be against us?" (Romans 8:31) God does not promise that he will deliver you according to your schedule or in the way you think is best. He merely says that he *will* deliver you. When you trust God, that promise is enough. When you know that your deliverance is assured, you can have patience and wait for it to be revealed.

YOU WILL GLORIFY GOD

When God does deliver you from adversity, you'll be changed by the experience. Your faith in him will be confirmed and your confidence in him will be stronger than ever. As a result you will offer spontaneous praise to him. "I will deliver thee, and thou shalt glorify me." That honoring of God is likely to take shape in several ways.

First, you will want to praise God for what he has done. When he lifts you up out of the dungeon, snaps your fetters, and makes a way through the difficulties that had seemed to be impossibilities, you will certainly thank him for it. I like the way one saintly lady put it, "If Jesus really saved me, he will never hear the last of it!" Like David, who wrote many psalms of thanksgiving, you'll tell God over and over how grateful you are for his deliverance. You will honor God with your gratitude.

Second, you will honor God for his deliverance by the wonderful testimony you give of his faithfulness. Very few people who experience a great deliverance keep that news to themselves. They tell their friends and neighbors, they tell their coworkers, they tell everyone who will listen. If the story is dramatic enough, they may even go on television or write a book about it. When you have been saved from trouble and you know for sure that God is the one who helped you, you'll spread that news.

Third, you will honor God for his deliverance by growing in your faith. Deliverance is a life-changing experience. It deepens your faith and focuses your mind. After God saves you from trouble, you'll have even greater confidence in him. You'll be all the more convinced that he loves you and that he is willing and able to come to your rescue. Imagine the power that will give to your prayers. You will say, "He has been with me in six troubles, and I know he will be with me in the seventh." You will glorify him by demonstrating increased patience and confidence. Your serenity will be more deep and lasting, and you will be able to defy Satan's attempts to drive away your joy and steal your peace of mind.

Fourth, you will honor God by being more consecrated to him than you have ever been. You will live more and more for his glory. The more you realize what God has done for you, the more you will want to dedicate your life to him in return. Your entire life will become a testimony of praise to God.

When we call out to God in times of trouble, he answers in a real, personal way. God's response to us is always personal, positive, practical, and permanent. Our response to him will be to give him glory through our gratitude, our testimony to others, our transformed life, and our renewed devotion to him.

OUT OF THE DEPTHS

No one likes adversity. We avoid suffering if we can. Yet we know that we cannot call on God in our time of trouble if we are not in trouble to begin with. And he cannot deliver us from difficulty if we have no problems. The world is a harsh place, and trouble is bound to come upon us in one form or another. And when it does, we have a remedy. We have someone who both cares about our suffering and is able to do something about it. We have someone to call.

If you are suffering right now, your first choice must be to move forward, to believe that your choices determine your destiny and that you can choose to pursue victory. Your second choice must be to trust God enough to call on him for help. Do you trust God? Are you in a close relationship with him? Do you have confidence that he can and will deliver you?

It's time to make the call. Cry out to God, and he will deliver you. Then you will truly know what it is to praise his name.

◇

THE SUCCESSFUL SEVEN

- List the reasons that you resist calling out to God and examine them in light of God's Word.

- Name the specific obstacles in your life that you know to be beyond your strength.

- Examine your heart. What is the current state of your relationship with God? If you were to call out to him right now, would he hear you?

- If your relationship with God has drifted to apathy or formality, confess that and ask that God will renew your close communion.

- List the daily practices that will keep your relationship with God active and growing.

- Call out to God for help. Pray sincerely, from your heart and without any pretense.

- Memorize Psalm 50:15.

◇

3
The Importance of a God Moment

Be still, and know that I am God.
—Psalm 46:10

THE WINNING CHOICE

I choose to develop a relationship with God.

THE POWER OF A MOMENT

A single moment of your time can dramatically alter your future. If you doubt that, consider the case of David Wagner. Wagner refers to himself as a *Daymaker*, meaning he is someone who makes people's day. While that may be his mission in life, Wagner for many years earned a living as a hairstylist and salon owner. One day he was working in his salon when a regular customer came in asking for a same-day appointment. She asked for her hair to be styled rather than simply cut, which was unusual for her. Wagner figured the woman must have had a social engagement that evening.

"No, I don't have anything special going on," she said. "I just want to look and feel good tonight."

Although she hadn't called ahead, Wagner was able to fit the woman into the schedule, and he spent the afternoon giving her the special treatment. "I was in a great mood that day and I was really 'on,'" he said. "I gave her a great scalp massage and shampoo like I always did and then styled her hair. We had a blast the whole time." When the styling was finished—along with the laughing and conversation that went along with it—the customer gave Wagner a hug that lasted just a bit longer than usual, then left.

Two days later, the salon owner received a letter from the woman. She related that she had come in that day because she had been planning to commit suicide and wanted her hair done so it would look good for the funeral. But during the hair appointment, she had changed her mind. She explained that Wagner had helped her see that life could be better, so she called her sister to talk about what she was going through. He sister took her to the hospital. That hair appointment saved her life.[12]

Yes, it is true. A single moment of your time, spent in the right company, can change your life. And if that is true for a depressed woman visiting her hairstylist, imagine the potentially life-changing effect of spending time with the God who created you, loves you, and has promised that your life will be better than it is right now. A moment spent with God can help you break free from the problems that keep you bound and create real momentum for growth. All God needs is a moment of your time. With that, he can change everything.

---

12. David Wagner, *My Life as a Daymaker: How to Change the World by Making Someone's Day* (San Diego, CA: Jodere Group, 2003), 2–3.

So far, you have made the choice to be an overcomer, and you have chosen to trust God by calling out to him for help. Now you face a third critical choice on your road from bondage to freedom. You must choose to spend time with the God who has the power to set you free.

HAMSTRUNG

Infertility has long been a source of heartache for married couples who long to become parents. In biblical times, the concept of infertility was used to indicate something beyond childlessness. Usually referred to as *barrenness*, the condition was sometimes understood in a symbolic sense to indicate suffering or adversity in a more general way. When people were unable to conceive or animals could not reproduce or land would not yield a harvest, people suffered. Thus, barrenness in Scripture is sometimes a shorthand description of the suffering of the entire nation of Israel. For example, when the prophet Isaiah says, "Sing, O barren, thou that didst not bear" (Isaiah 54:1), he is really speaking to Israel as a whole; he's talking about the "barrenness" of the nation. Barrenness is an awful thing. To be barren is to be empty, ineffective, or powerless.

Interestingly, the Hebrew word for *barren* is also the root of a verb meaning to make unfit or to hamstring. If you have ever had an injury to the hamstring muscles on the back of your thigh, you know how painful and frustrating that can be. When animals are hamstrung, the tendons on the back of their leg are severed, causing them to limp. To be hamstrung is to be limited, unable to move freely. Both concepts—to be barren and to be hamstrung—illustrate the effect of adversity in our lives. It leaves us empty and paralyzed.

You can be hamstrung in life because of a disappointment in a relationship. You may be hamstrung by your false expectations. You may be hamstrung by placing your faith in people who later let you down. You may be left empty and immobile by taking on too many obligations. Athletes know that careful stretching is required prior to exercise to avoid injuring the hamstring. But like undisciplined athletes, we sometimes hamstring ourselves through our poor choices or inattention to our spiritual lives.

A hamstring injury is one of the most frustrating an athlete can incur because it restricts movement but does not eliminate it. When your hamstring is injured, you can still walk and perhaps even run, but not very well. You limp along, unable to reach your true potential. That may be your condition right now because of the adversity you face. It has left you restricted, slowed, held back. You're in a difficult marriage, perhaps, and that leaves you running at half-speed in every area of life. Perhaps you have lost your job. Now nothing else seems to make sense. You can move a little, but you cannot move forward as you would like. What will you do next? What therapy can you apply to that damaged muscle? How can you move beyond the barren (empty) place where you are?

Returning to Isaiah 54, we see the prophet's advice to Israel. "Sing, O barren, thou that didst not bear; break forth into singing, and cry aloud, thou that didst not travail with child: for more are the children of the desolate than the children of the married wife, saith the Lord" (Isaiah 54:1). Isaiah's advice? Break forth in singing. Worship. Spending even a little time in the presence of God will change your outlook, renew your strength, and transform your future.

It's possible that you have become so used to nursing your injury—that is, to living with your adversity—that you have stopped looking for positive steps that will lead to your deliverance. It's time to move beyond that, and Isaiah gives us a simple admonition for moving forward. Switch from sorrow to singing. Stop thinking about your problems and start focusing on your Potentate. Get your mind into a framework of worship. Spend some time with your heavenly Father and begin to see life from his perspective. You need a moment alone with God. That moment will change your life.

TIME ALONE WITH GOD

Spending time with God is a powerful practice, as any of the great spiritual masters of church history can attest. Jesus himself is our example in this practice, for we know that he often "withdrew himself into the wilderness, and prayed" (Luke 5:16). Spending time with the Father wasn't a humdrum part of Jesus' daily routine. He used this time strategically to gain the Father's perspective and steel himself against the demands of ministry. For example, Jesus spent the entire night in prayer before making one of his most critical decisions, selecting the twelve apostles (Luke 6:12). On the fateful night of his arrest, Jesus withdrew with his apostles to pray in the garden of Gethsemane. It was there that he prayed, "Nevertheless not my will, but thine, be done," finding the courage to carry his mission through to the end (Luke 22:42). Before one of his most powerful miracles, multiplying the loaves and fish, Jesus looked up to heaven and gave thanks to the Father (Matthew 14:19). Jesus knew the source of his strength. It came from those moments of secret communion.

If Jesus depended on regular, intimate time with the Father in order to move forward with his mission, how much more do you need daily time in the presence of God? How can you hope to break free from your circumstances, overcome your adversity, or gain momentum without the daily practice of spending time with your heavenly Father?

This time spent with God is rejuvenating, but it's more than that. It is a power connection that enables you to move forward. Remember what Jesus said about the power of prayer. "Ask, and it shall be given you; seek, and ye shall find; knock, and it shall be opened unto you" (Matthew 7:7). "And all things, whatsoever ye shall ask in prayer, believing, ye shall receive" (Matthew 21:22). "Therefore I say unto you, What things soever ye desire, when ye pray, believe that ye receive them, and ye shall have them" (Mark 11:24). Prayer will make you feel better, there's no doubt. It will also avail you of the resources you need to move forward. There is power in prayer.

One person who knew the power of time spent with God was Corrie ten Boom, a Dutch woman who was imprisoned along with her sister, Betsie, in the Ravensbrück concentration camp for hiding Jewish refugees during World War II. The sisters braved captivity, starvation, and disease yet had the courage to lead others in worship using a Bible that had been smuggled into the camp. Those times of worship sustained the sisters through their darkest hours. Betsie died in prison and before her death told Corrie, "[We] must tell people what we have learned here. We must tell them that there is no pit so deep that He is not deeper still."[13] The sisters understood that regardless of the adversity we face or the

13. Corrie ten Boom with Elizabeth and John Sherrill, *The Hiding Place* (Peabody, MA: Hendrickson Publishers, 2009), 240.

difficult situations we find ourselves in, God's presence will carry us through.

In later years, Corrie became a well-known international speaker, and she spoke of the power of worship to banish doubt and fear. She wrote, "I knew from experience what to do when the demon fear entered my heart. He had called on me many a time during my imprisonment in Germany, and I would then begin to sing. Singing always helps. Try it yourself sometime; fear and anxiety will vanish when you sing."[14]

She might have been quoting Isaiah, "Sing, O barren, thou that didst not bear; break forth into singing, and cry aloud" (Isaiah 54:1). When you are stuck in the mire of suffering, hemmed in by your circumstances, doubts, and fears, lift your voice in worship of God. A single moment in his presence will renew your mind, lift your spirits, and set you on the road to recovery. Worship has the power to break you free from the forces that hold you back.

THE POWER SOURCE

Some of the things we use every day are a bit of a mystery, even though they are familiar. For example, an electrical engineer will tell you that nobody knows exactly how or why electrical energy travels along a wire. We know only that it does. We can start it, stop it, and harness its effects, even though we can't explain exactly how it works. You may not understand electricity, but you still use it every day to light your home, power your computer, and start your car. You don't have to know why it works in order to benefit from it.

Personal worship is something like that. You don't have to know why praising God changes your heart in order to experience

---

14. Corrie ten Boom, *Amazing Love: True Stories of the Power of Forgiveness* (Washington, PA: CLC Publications, 2011), 61.

that transformation. You don't have to know how prayer operates in order to benefit from it. When you spend time with your heavenly Father, you benefit from his presence and power in ways that you likely can't fully explain. A moment alone with him will change your heart, enlarge your vision for the future, and prompt you to take action. Here are some of the simple things you can do to spend time with God and some of the ways that experience will help you through the adversity you face right now.

PRAISE: IT WILL SHIFT YOUR FOCUS

One of the reasons we remain stuck in our current circumstances is that we focus too much attention on them. When all you can see is your problems, you will have very little imagination or creativity to envision solutions. One benefit of time with the Lord is that it shifts your focus away from what's wrong and toward what's right. You begin to take your eyes off your problems and see your Potentate. And when you get a vision of who God is, you will see your own life more clearly too.

That's what happened to Isaiah. At the time Isaiah began his ministry, the nation of Israel was in crisis. King Uzziah had just passed away, a powerful king who had led Israel for more than fifty years. Such moments of transition are unsettling for any nation and can even prompt a national emergency. It was then, in the year that King Uzziah died, that Isaiah had his vision of God. Isaiah writes, "I saw also the LORD sitting upon a throne, high and lifted up, and his train filled the temple" (Isaiah 6:1). Isaiah goes on to describe a vision of the heavenly creatures worshiping and praising God: "Holy, holy, holy, is the LORD of hosts: the whole earth is full of his glory" (verse 3). What an experience! When you get a glimpse of who God is—powerful, holy, righteous, good, just, omniscient, perfect—it will change your life.

In your moment with God, praise him. Affirm that he is the one, righteous, all-knowing, all-powerful God. Read the Psalms, many of which are rich songs of praise. Thank God for who he is and what he has done. Meditate on his name and on his many titles and descriptions found in Scripture, such as Mighty God, Most High, Provider, and Creator. Sing your praise using favorite hymns or gospel songs. You cannot praise God and be overwhelmed by your problems at the same time. Let the experience of worship lift your sights away from the hopelessness of your circumstances to the all-powerful Creator. If you've been complaining about your problems, your solution is to start singing. When you magnify God, you minimize yourself and your suffering.

SURRENDER: IT WILL HEAL YOUR BROKENNESS

Surrender is an act of worship that places you—your whole life, body, mind, and spirit—before the Lord. This is what Paul spoke of in Romans 12:1: "I beseech you therefore, brethren, by the mercies of God, that ye present your bodies a living sacrifice, holy, acceptable unto God, which is your reasonable service." Paul was alluding to the practice of animal sacrifice, in which cattle and other animals were literally put to death and placed upon an altar. Our spiritual sacrifice is similar in that it involves a kind of dying, giving up everything to God—your heart, mind, will, emotions, all that you are. It is letting go and saying, "Lord, I am 100 percent yours, problems and all."

When you surrender to God at a deep level, you will find that something amazing happens. The hurts in your life begin to heal. Rather than holding on to them, rationalizing your own actions and holding grudges against other people, you begin to experi-ence freedom. You find the grace and courage to forgive others. You stop protecting your ego and start letting God work on your soul. You find that you have become stronger at the broken places.

There is something powerful about breaking, and God blesses things that have been broken. When a little boy gave Jesus two fish and five loaves of bread, the first thing he did was break the bread. It had to be broken before it could be blessed, multiplied, and used. When you refuse to surrender to God, you're actually refusing to be broken in the places of your heart that you reserve only for yourself. You're refusing to surrender your pride and sin. And by this refusal, you hold on to the hurts of the past, trying to nurse them yourself instead of allowing God to heal them.

God will bless your broken places if you will surrender them to him. When you have your moment with the Lord, be com-pletely open. Don't be afraid of the Spirit's touch. There may be painful places in your life and places you fear surrendering fully to God. Have faith. Give yourself fully to God. You'll be amazed at what he gives you in return.

REPENT: IT WILL BREAK OPEN THE HARD PLACES

Sometimes soil becomes compacted and compressed after a heavy rain. The ground becomes hard, so hard that it can no lon-ger soak up moisture or accept new seed. Hardened soil will choke the oxygen out of any plant that tries to sprout there. When the ground becomes hard, there is only one solution: it must be bro-ken up. The farmer must plow up the hard ground, sometimes more than once, to break up the clots and aerate the soil. Only then will the land become fertile again, a place where new life can begin.

Adversity has a way of compacting the soil of the heart. When you suffer adversity of any kind, your reaction may be to retreat into yourself, becoming closed to God and others. You may even adopt some coping strategies that are unhealthy, like using alcohol or drugs, overindulging in food, or gossiping in an attempt to feel better about yourself. Before long, those patterns become sinful habits. Your heart is hardened. You are trapped in a lifestyle that keeps you bound. You must break up the hard ground through repentance.

Repentance is turning away from what's wrong and toward what's right. It is a change of heart that leads to a change of behavior. Before Jesus began his public ministry, John the Baptist called the people to repent. They needed a change of heart before they could accept the good news. We read about that in Mark 1:2–5:

> As it is written in the prophets, Behold, I send my messenger before thy face, which shall prepare thy way before thee. The voice of one crying in the wilderness, Prepare ye the way of the Lord, make his paths straight. John did baptize in the wilderness, and preach the baptism of repentance for the remission of sins. And there went out unto him all the land of Judaea, and they of Jerusalem, and were all baptized of him in the river Jordan, confessing their sins.

John's mission was to break up the hard ground, creating openness in the people so they could hear and accept the message of the Messiah. Repentance breaks open hard hearts so new growth can take place.

In your time with God, take a chisel to the hard places in your life. Allow the Spirit to search you so that you can see where you need to change. Be open to the Spirit's leading. Don't allow any area to remain closed. Bring everything out into the light of day. This is a process of self-evaluation, directed by the Spirit. Ask yourself, "Why am I not seeing God move in my life? Is there something within me that is blocking the movement of the Spirit?" Then listen for the Spirit's response. Confess the sin that God reveals to you. Tell him that you are sorry for rebelling against his will, then accept God's forgiveness. When you do, your heart will be tender, open, and ready for what comes next.

AGREE: IT WILL STRENGTHEN YOUR FAITH

When Isaiah told the barren one to sing, he wasn't suggesting that she whistle through the graveyard, ignoring the facts and pretending that she didn't have problems. The prophet was trying to show that the blessing of God had already been pronounced, so people could rejoice about the future God had already established. Read this passage closely: "Sing, O barren, thou that didst not bear; break forth into singing, and cry aloud, thou that didst not travail with child: *for more are the children of the desolate than the children of the married wife*, saith the LORD" (Isaiah 54:1, emphasis added). The emphasized portion is a reference to the future, not the present. Isaiah points out that the "barren" woman will someday have even more children than the married wife has now. The people who are suffering, barren, hamstrung, will soon be blessed in great measure—so rejoice!

When you accept God's Word as true, agreeing with him about the certainty of his promises, you open yourself to possibilities you had not previously considered. As long as you focus on what's wrong—what didn't happen, what should have happened, what can't happen—you will never see the beautiful possibilities of God's promise. Your lack of faith will shut you out of that blessing. However, when you lift your voice in praise, affirming the good and precious promises that God has given, you open yourself to those possibilities. Faith opens the door to a better future.

In your moment with the Lord, listen. Be silent long enough to let God speak to you. Stop complaining so that you can hear his voice. Meditate on the Word. List the promises that God has given you as part of the household of faith. Then name the promises that God has revealed to you personally. State them. Then affirm them. Believe them. Rely on them.

ENVISION: IT WILL CREATE A NEW REALITY

A vision is a description of the future as it can be, as it will be through God's grace. Nearly all of Isaiah 54 is a vision of the future, but two verses paint that vision in especially vivid terms: "For thou shalt break forth on the right hand and on the left; and thy seed shall inherit the Gentiles, and make the desolate cities to be inhabited. Fear not; for thou shalt not be ashamed: neither be thou confounded; for thou shalt not be put to shame: for thou shalt forget the shame of thy youth, and shalt not remember the reproach of thy widowhood any more" (Isaiah 54:3–4).

Notice two things about this vision. First, the future will be much different than the present. Isaiah prophesied that Israel would inherit the nations, and that cities that were desolate would become thriving population centers. The future, he says, will look nothing like the current reality. Second, notice that the future will be different than the past. The people will forget the former shame they felt. Their embarrassment at being "barren" will disappear. The old, bitter times will melt away. Better days are ahead.

Time spent with God will impress a positive vision on your heart. When you see God for who he is, offer yourself fully and freely to him, and agree with his assessment of the situation, you begin to see the future as it will be through God's grace. During your moment with the Lord, allow yourself to dream. Ask the Lord to plant a new vision in your mind. Lift your sights to see the world as he sees it. Ask, "Lord, what new thing do you have for me?"

ACT: IT WILL GENERATE MOMENTUM

A breakthrough is an act or action that breaks through an obstruction or restriction, often suddenly and with great force. The Israelites crossing the Red Sea experienced a breakthrough. They had been trapped with no way to escape the Egyptian army. Yet the Lord parted the waters so the people crossed through on dry ground. The capture of Jericho was a breakthrough. The city was shut up tight with no way in or out. Then, after six days of marching around the city in silence, the Israelites marched on the seventh day and, on the seventh circuit, raised a great shout. With that, the walls collapsed—a literal breakthrough. The day of Pentecost was a spiritual breakthrough as the Spirit came with power upon the believers who were huddled together in one place. What you need to move beyond the forces that restrain you is a breakthrough of God's power applied to your situation.

Notice that in every instance of breakthrough, there was communication with God followed by action. God met with Moses and told him to hold out his staff over the sea. When Moses did that, the waters parted. God directed the Israelites to march around the city, and as they marched the walls fell. Jesus commanded the believers to wait in Jerusalem, and then the Spirit came. When they were filled with the Holy Ghost, they spoke in tongues and preached the Word with conviction and power. A moment with God followed by obedient action produces a breakthrough.

After you have had your moment with God—praising, submitting, repenting, affirming, envisioning—you must take action. You must put deeds behind the vision you have received from the Lord. The breakthrough will come as you rise, go, and put into practice what God has revealed to you.

Let's return to Isaiah 54. We have read that the Lord promised times of abundance would soon come, symbolized by a barren woman producing many children. That was the promise. And we see also the action God directed: "Enlarge the place of thy tent, and let them stretch forth the curtains of thine habitations: spare not, lengthen thy cords, and strengthen thy stakes" (Isaiah 54:2). In effect, God is saying, "Get yourself a bigger house. You need more bedrooms and a larger yard, because you're going to have a lot of children!" He urged the people to take immediate action to prepare for the blessing that would soon follow.

When God gives you a vision, don't sit on your hands. Don't remain stuck when he has shown you the way forward. Begin now to prepare for the promise. This does not mean to act foolishly or impulsively. It's easy to get ahead of the Lord's timing by being impetuous. If God has promised you prosperity, that doesn't mean you should borrow money today because you know God will repay it next year. It means that you should learn to manage well so you'll be able to handle the blessing when it comes. If God has shown you that you will further your education, that doesn't mean you should quit your job tomorrow. It may mean that you should begin to downsize your possessions so you will be ready to move when the time comes. The basic idea is to take action in the direction that God has called you to move. When he says, "It's time to go," don't be caught sitting on your hands. If he has promised the blessing of rain, get your shovel and dig some ditches. Position yourself to be ready for God's deliverance.

When you begin to move in concert with God's direction, you will experience momentum. That momentum will enable you to overcome the resistance in your life. You'll get a taste of what David was talking about when he said, "With your help I can advance against a troop; with my God I can scale a wall" (2 Samuel 22:30 NIV). When the gate opens, move through it. Don't complain that you are hemmed in by your circumstances. Let your moment with God take you beyond your present limitations. You cannot build momentum without movement. You cannot steer a ship that is standing still. To change direction, you must do something to generate forward progress. You must take action.

A MOMENT IN TIME

Perhaps you've heard someone use the expression, "I just need a moment," or "I'm having a moment." They're not talking about a minute or two of literal time. In those contexts, *moment* refers to a particular experience at an opportune time. When a politician has his "moment," it means that he has his time in the spotlight. A "moment of truth" is a defining event, one that decides a critical question. So when we speak of a moment with God, we're not talking about five minutes. To have a moment with God is to have a meaningful, intimate experience of him that is timely for your situation. It is a moment in which God breaks into your current reality with his presence and power, transforming your mind, your heart, and your outlook on the future. That moment may come in a flash, or it may be the result of days, or even months of patiently seeking God through worship. One thing is certain however, your moment will not happen by accident. You must choose your moment. You must seize your moment. You must be intentional about having personal communion with the heavenly Father.

To have a moment with God, you must do something more than simply be available. You must seek the Lord. Some people think that since God knows everything, he must know where they are and is therefore welcome to come and spend time with them anytime he desires. "I'll be here watching TV as usual," they say to God. "Feel free to interrupt me whenever you'd like to talk." But God doesn't work that way. Very rarely will God interrupt you when you are focused on something else. To have a moment with God, you must pursue him through purposeful activities like prayer, daily quiet time, Sunday worship, small group time, and prayer meetings. Never underestimate the power of a season of prayer. Do not overlook the value of a single worship service. Heed the call of the prophet Isaiah and "seek ye the LORD while he may be found, call ye upon him while he is near" (Isaiah 55:6). Pursue God with all your heart. Create the opportunity to have a moment with him. Remember, a moment with God will cause you to move beyond the forces that have hamstrung you. A moment with God will change your life. Don't let that moment pass you by.

◇

THE SUCCESSFUL SEVEN

- Name the time and place where you will daily spend time alone with God.

- Determine now that you will attend worship each week; make this a single decision rather than fifty-two decisions each year.

- List five reasons that you have to praise God.

- Spend time in prayer asking God to reveal hidden sins or blockages in your life.

- Ask the Lord, "What vision do you have for my life?" Then wait for his answer.

- Write down the next action you will take to create momentum in your life.

- Memorize Psalm 46:10.

◇

4

You Need a Word from God

Study to shew thyself approved unto God,
a workman that needeth not to be ashamed,
rightly dividing the word of truth.
—2 Timothy 2:15

THE WINNING CHOICE

I choose to obey God.

FACT VS. FICTION

Few events are as laden with emotions and expectations as a wedding. From the tearful parents of the bride and groom to the joyful friends and relatives to the beaming-yet-overwrought couple, a marriage ceremony may be the most emotional of all events. One reason emotions run so high is that we bring so many preconceived notions to the experience. Every bride and groom have a picture-perfect vision for their wedding. Generally, that begins with a lovely, flawlessly executed ceremony conducted on a bright, clear day, followed by a joyous reception hosting perpetually smiling friends and loved ones, then jetting away to a hotel balcony and staring lovingly into one another's eyes while listening to the surf crash gently upon the beach. That's a lovely vision, and it's easy to become so preoccupied with it that we lose sight of the fact that a wedding is an ordinary event involving people, food, weather, and emotions—a most unpredictable combination. Regardless of the planning involved, when our high expectations collide with stark reality, emotions may spin out of control. I wonder how many brides wind up in tears on their wedding night?

Actually, we know the answer to that. In an informal survey conducted by *Bride*, 9 percent of newlyweds confessed to spending their first night in tears. Others had more humorous experiences that nevertheless demonstrate how far our sentimental vision can be from reality. Seven in 10 brides said they spent most of their first night removing pins and clips from their intricate hairdos. Two-thirds passed the entire evening with family and friends rather than sneaking away for some alone time. More than 20 percent of couples spent their time opening presents and counting cash. Five couples surveyed wound up spending time at the emergency room, and one pair of newlyweds, upon discovering that their hotel offered free use of a washer and dryer, spent the whole night doing laundry to save money![15] Clearly, our romantic notions of the wedding experience don't always match reality. This is one matter about which we are informed less by facts than by feelings.

15. Andrea Magrath, "Updating Facebook relationship statuses, counting their cash, trips to the emergency room and doing laundry: Couples confess how they really spent their wedding night," *Daily Mail* website, May 7, 2015, http://www. dailymail.co.uk/femail/article-3072804/Updating-Facebook-relationship-statuses-counting-cash-trips-emergency-room-doing-laundry-Couples-confess-REALLY-spent-wedding-night.html.

In a similar way, our vision of life as followers of Jesus may be more sentimental than factual. Our view of the Christian experience is often shaped by our emotions. As a result, we can easily be pulled away from our identity in Christ and miss out on the work of the Spirit in our lives.

You have made the decision to be an overcomer, displayed your faith by calling upon God for help, and committed to the daily practice of praise and worship. You are well on your way to living as an overcomer. However, that progress may be derailed if your view of the Christian life is based on emotion rather than fact. So the fourth critical decision you must make to win over adversity is to base your life on the Word. You must choose to know God's Word so that it shapes your identity and activates the work of the Spirit in your life.

BEYOND EMOTIONAL FAITH

Emotion is part of the Christian experience; there is no question about that. When God saves us from our sin, we are elated. When the Spirit moves on us with power, we become excited. When we see injustice and the effects of sin upon people, we are angry. If you have never had an occasion where the joy of the Holy Ghost has gripped your heart, causing you to sing, shout, or dance with delight, then I pray you will. It is a wonderful thing to be touched by God in a way that produces joy.

However, for too many Christians, emotion is all there is to the faith. Having once been moved by the Spirit during worship, they wrongly conclude that the mountaintop experience is the norm. Rather than seeing such high moments as a glimpse of the Spirit's power, a window into heaven, they conclude that emotion should be the engine that drives their day-to-day experience.

When that emotion evaporates and the mountaintop gives way to the valley, they find themselves stuck. Their emotion-only faith does not have the power to deal with rejection, sadness, boredom, or adversity. To compensate, they often chase that feeling by running from conference to conference or from church to church, hoping that the next speaker or worship leader can help them recover that lost feeling. Some just give up trying to grow spiritually, settling for an impotent faith. They choose to remain stuck.

No person felt the emotions of faith more keenly than Jesus did. He felt compassion for those who suffered (Matthew 9:36). He experienced anger at the misuse of the temple in his day (Mark 11:17), and he grieved over the city of Jerusalem (Luke 19:41–44). Jesus loved Lazarus (John 11:36) and wept over his death (John 11:35). Jesus also rejoiced in the Spirit (Luke 10:21), not a tepid smile but an ecstatic celebration! To be human is to experience emotion, and Christians have the same range of emotions as anyone else. We experience them vividly because of our deep spirit-to-Spirit connection with the Creator.

Yet it is possible to have too much emotion and not enough instruction. We need a faith that is grounded in the truth of the Word, not on the shifting sands of our feelings. And we see this doctrinal grounding in the life and ministry of our Lord. His life was deeply rooted in the Word. We can observe the power of this Word-centered life played out in a series of events recorded in Luke 4. The key verse for understanding this series of events and how they apply to your life is Luke 4:36: "And they were all amazed, and spake among themselves, saying, What a word is this! for with authority and power he commandeth the unclean spirits, and they come out." Jesus knew the Word, and he spoke it with authority, and the Word exercised great power in his life. If you are to win over adversity, to move beyond the obstacles that now hold you back, you must move beyond an emotional faith to be grounded in the Word of God. You must know the Word and use it in your daily life. Let's see how that works, using the life of Jesus as our example.

THE WORD OF TRUTH: VICTORY OVER TEMPTATION

Immediately after his baptism (see Luke 3:21–22), Jesus was led by the Spirit into the wilderness for a time of testing. Three times the devil came to Jesus with an offer that sounded appealing in some way but was really a compromise of his principles. Jesus was hungry, and the devil suggested that Jesus use his power for his own gratification by transforming stones into bread. That small act of self-protection would have compromised Jesus' ability to sacrifice his life for others.

Jesus' mission was to proclaim the good news of the kingdom of God (Luke 4:43), a mission that he later entrusted to all his followers at the Great Commission (Matthew 28:19–20). So the devil's next ploy was to show Jesus all the kingdoms of the world and offer to place them in his hands. The price? Jesus would have to break faith by worshiping Satan. This end-justifies-the-means thinking would have meant taking the easy way out. It would have destroyed Jesus' moral authority.

Finally, the devil took Jesus to the pinnacle of the temple and urged him to cast himself down so that angels would come to his rescue. To do so would have proven to everyone that Jesus was who he claimed to be, though it would have meant misusing his power. Jesus faced this temptation again and again as people constantly asked him for some sort of sign to prove his identity. To give in to this would have placed Jesus under the authority of others; he would have been people pleasing for the rest of his ministry.

In each case, Jesus responded by citing the Word of God. In response to the first temptation, Jesus said, "Man shall not live by bread alone, but by every word of God" (Luke 4:4), a reference to Deuteronomy 8:3. To the second, he replied, "Get thee behind me, Satan: for it is written, Thou shalt worship the Lord thy God, and him only shalt thou serve" (Luke 4:8), a quotation of Deuteronomy 6:13. And to the third offer, Jesus said, "Thou shalt not tempt the Lord thy God" (Luke 4:12), citing Deuteronomy 6:16. Jesus, the Living Word, had a powerful command of the written Word, the Scriptures. And he used that knowledge to fend off the subtle schemes of the devil that were designed as a snare for him. Had Jesus fallen for any of those temptations, he would have compromised his mission. The Word gave him victory over temptation.

When your experience of God is purely emotional, you will be vulnerable to temptation because you'll be in the habit of following your volatile emotions wherever they lead. When you're hungry, that hunger will seem like your most pressing concern. When you are angry—either righteously angry or simply peeved at another person—that irritation will dominate your thoughts. When you are focused on a goal, that focus will become all consuming. Even your elation may pull you off course as you are tempted to celebrate in selfish or destructive ways. Having an intellectual grounding in the Word is your defense against doing whatever feels right in the moment. When you know the Word, you have a standard for judging what is best. You won't be dependent on emotion alone.

For example, when you know the Word, you know that satisfying your own needs may feel like the most pressing concern, but caring for others must come first. "Look not every man on his own things, but every man also on the things of others" (Philippians 2:4). When you are driven by emotion, you may take every negative event in your life as proof that God has abandoned you. You will be subject to discouragement at every turn. When you know the Word, you will realize that nothing can separate you from God's presence. "If I ascend up into heaven, thou art there: if I make my bed in hell, behold, thou art there" (Psalm 139:8). When you are grounded in the Word, you have the ability to discern truth from error so you won't be easily confused by false teaching. You won't be "tossed to and fro, and carried about with every wind of doctrine" (Ephesians 4:14). Emotion-based faith leaves you vulnerable to temptation. It will result in repeating the same old mistakes that got you stuck in the first place. If you want to win over adversity, you must know the Word. The sword of the Spirit, which is the Word of God, is your weapon for winning over temptation.

THE WORD OF AFFIRMATION: VICTORY OVER REJECTION

The second episode in Luke 4 concerns an experience that every one of us has suffered or will suffer. Jesus suffered it too. That experience is rejection. You may be facing rejection right now, such as the painful rejection of a broken marriage. Joblessness is another form of rejection in that you may feel no one values you or the contribution you can make. Failure of any kind brings feelings of isolation and rejection. Other things like illness or financial woes or poor grades can feel like a form of rejection because they separate you from other people socially. Rejection is always painful. It's one of the things that hamstrings us, making it hard to move forward and realize our potential.

Jesus experienced rejection in the last place we might expect it, among his own people in his hometown of Nazareth. After his testing in the desert, Jesus returned to Nazareth "in the power of the Spirit" (Luke 4:14). And when he got there, he went to the synagogue on the Sabbath day, as he always did, and read a passage from the prophet Isaiah. Then he said, "This day is this scripture fulfilled in your ears" (verse 21). It was a way of saying, "The time has come! God's kingdom starts now!" It should have sounded like exciting news, and it did at first. Everybody commented on how well Jesus spoke, and they were quite amazed. But then the feeling shifted. People began to say, "Wait a minute. I know this guy. This is Joseph's son." When the people realized that Jesus was a hometown boy who had come back as a powerful rabbi, they were less impressed. After a tense exchange with Jesus, the crowd became furious and actually tried to throw him off a cliff (verse 29). Talk about rejection! Fortunately, Jesus slipped through their hands and went on his way.

Jesus experienced rejection by the very people who should have been the most open to him—his own people. As John put it, "He came unto his own, and his own received him not" (John 1:11). This was a painful thing for Jesus to bear. We know that because later in his ministry Jesus wept over the failure of the Jewish people to accept his message. Luke writes, "And when he was come near [Jerusalem], he beheld the city, and wept over it, Saying, If thou hadst known, even thou, at least in this thy day, the things which belong unto thy peace! but now they are hid from thine eyes" (Luke 19:41–42).

Yet Jesus' experience of rejection did not derail his ministry. He continued on, taking the message to those who were open to it. How did he have the inner strength to bear the emotional pain, something most of us find so hard to do? The answer is found in the happening that immediately precedes the events of Luke 4, Jesus' baptism.

Before Jesus began his ministry, he was baptized in the Jordan River by John the Baptist (see Luke 3:21–22). At that time, while Jesus was praying, heaven opened and the Holy Spirit descended on him in bodily form, like a dove. A voice came from heaven saying: "Thou art my beloved Son; in thee I am well pleased" (verse 22). There in the Jordan River, Jesus received a word of affirmation. His identity was declared for all to hear. That word of affirmation grounded Jesus' identity. It gave him the strength to endure the conflict and rejection that characterized so much of his ministry. Everyone needs affirmation. We all thrive on it. And it was important for Jesus to begin his ministry with this affirmation of his identity. He rose up from the Jordan like the Israelites who crossed that same river centuries earlier, strengthened for the days to follow.

If your faith is based on feelings, you will have no emotional reserves to carry you through the emotional pain of rejection. No matter how much we may say that we don't care what people think of us, we really do care. We all need affirmation. We were built to receive it. So it is vital to hear the affirmation of the Father, to have that affirmation descend on you like a dove, quieting your spirit and giving you strength. In order to receive that affirmation, you must be grounded in the Word of God, for it is there that your identity is established. Here are just a few of the things the Word of God says about you as his child. You are—

- Chosen (Ephesians 1:4)

- Forgiven (Ephesians 1:6–8)

- Loved (Romans 8:39)

- Accepted (Romans 15:7)

- A Child of God (John 1:12)

- A Child of Promise (Galatians 4:28)

- A Friend of God (John 15:14)

- God's Handiwork (Ephesians 2:10)

- Holy (Matthew 27:52)

- The Light of the World (Matthew 5:14–16)

- A New Creation (2 Corinthians 5:17)

When you experience adversity, listen to the affirmation of God's Word. If you want to make it through the wilderness seasons in your life, especially times of rejection, you will need that affirmation to sustain you. It will remind you of your identity, your calling, and your purpose. And remember this: to be rejected in one place is to be accepted in another. Jesus may have been rejected by his own people, but he was accepted by those who had ears to hear the truth. When you are rejected on earth, you are accepted in heaven. You may not understand the reasons for what you experience now, but when you get to the other side, you will find the place where it is written, "The Spirit of the Lord is upon me, because he hath anointed me" (Luke 4:18). Like Jesus, you will know that God's Spirit rests on you despite what others may say.

Often, the rejection we experience at the hands of others propels us to a prophetic future. That was true for Joseph, who was cruelly rejected by his brothers, even sold as a slave. However, that rejection served a greater purpose. Later in his life, he was able to say to his brothers, "You intended to harm me, but God intended it for good to accomplish what is now being done, the saving of many lives" (Genesis 50:20 NIV). When you experience rejection by people who oppose God's will, take it as a sign that you are headed in the right direction. Joseph, Moses, David, Jesus—all were rejected. Yet all weathered that rejection because they understood that their identity was determined not by what other people said about them but by the Word of God.

When you lack the affirmation of your identity and purpose that comes from the Word of God, you will be stuck looking for that affirmation from other people. Sometimes they will affirm you, and sometimes they won't. So you'll be tossed back and forth, never able to rise above the negative feelings that come with rejection. What's worse, when you do receive affirmation, it will be from the wrong source. It will be based on the vagaries of human opinion, not the solid foundation of God's Word. To win over adversity, you must have a strong sense of who you are, affirmed through the Word of God.

THE WORD OF AUTHORITY: VICTORY OVER THE ENEMY

Jesus moved on from his rejection at Nazareth to the nearby town of Capernaum, which became his home base for ministry. This was a fishing village on the shores of the Sea of Galilee, and it was the home of Peter, James, and John, Jesus' first disciples. It's interesting that Jesus went to Capernaum, which means *placated* or *appeased*. Capernaum may have been a sleepy little town where things were placid, but Jesus came to shake them up a bit! Jesus taught them on the Sabbath days, just as he had done in Nazareth, but the results could not have been more different. It was in Capernaum that people "were astonished at his doctrine: for his word was with power" (Luke 4:32). And on one Sabbath day, there was a man present who had an unclean spirit. The spirit cried out saying, "Let us alone; what have we to do with thee, thou Jesus of Nazareth? art thou come to destroy us? I know thee who thou art; the Holy One of God" (verse 34). Jesus commanded the spirit to leave the man and it did so immediately. Again, the people "were all amazed, and spake among themselves, saying, What a word is this! for with authority and power he commandeth the unclean spirits" (verse 36).

Jesus' teaching had great authority. He wasn't speaking so that everyone would say, "How nice," or, "Isn't that sweet." He spoke to bring change in the world and in people's lives. Even the demons recognized who he was and responded to his command. People could not help but notice that there was something different about this rabbi. He was not at all like the religious teachers of the day, who hemmed and hawed, citing a long history of religious tradition and the teachings of other rabbis before offering their opinion. Jesus told it like it was and he saw results from his teaching. Why? Because he was firmly grounded in the Word of truth, *and* he put that Word into practice.

The word *taught* here means to teach by both information and demonstration. It's not just telling but also showing. It's not just information and it's not just demonstration. It's both. Jesus spoke to the people (information) and he cast out demons (demonstrating his power). We need both doctrine and demonstration, pulled together and balanced. Principles are important, but they are nothing without power. Whatever we teach—or learn—must be demonstrated in life. This means that in order to be people of the Word, we must submit to the Word in all ways. We must not merely *know* the Word. We must do it also. We must put the Word into practice in our lives. As James says, "But be ye doers of the word, and not hearers only, deceiving your own selves" (James 1:22).

Adversity can serve a positive purpose in our lives by keeping us from getting complacent. Jesus went to Capernaum to comfort the afflicted but also to afflict the comfortable. A bit of adversity can focus our attention where it belongs—on God. However, Satan desires to destroy us through hardship, temptation, suffering, and other forms of adversity. When your faith is dependent on emotions, you'll never be able to move beyond adversity. You will remain stuck in whatever rut the devil places you because you don't have the strength, stamina, or spiritual authority to move forward. To break free, you must both understand the Word of God *and* submit to its authority by putting it into practice in your life.

If you are unwilling to submit to the Word, you're just fooling yourself. You will not experience God's power until you begin to apply his Word. You'll remain stuck. But when you submit to the Word by obeying it, you'll see God's deliverance emerge. God's authority does not rest on those who change their beliefs every week or two, or who affirm the truth only when they're in the right mood. His authority rests on those who know, trust, and practice his Word in every aspect of their lives. That means moving on from elementary things to deeper truths. As Isaiah says, "Whom shall he teach knowledge? and whom shall he make

to understand doctrine? them that are weaned from the milk"
(Isaiah 28:9).

Are you ready to move beyond your current circumstances?
Are you ready for God's power and authority to rest on you? Then
it's time to move beyond celebration and shouting—as valuable
as those experiences are—and apply the Word of God to your life.
You must begin to live out the meaning of texts like these:

- "Except a man be born of water and of the Spirit, he
  cannot enter into the kingdom of God" (John 3:5).

- "Bring ye all the tithes into the storehouse"
  (Malachi 3:10).

- "A new commandment I give unto you, That ye love
  one another" (John 13:34).

- "Receive ye the Holy Ghost" (John 20:22).

- "Go ye therefore, and teach all nations, baptizing them
  in the name of the Father, and of the Son, and of the
  Holy Ghost: Teaching them to observe all things whatsoever I have commanded you" (Matthew 28:19–20).

- "Not forsaking the assembling of ourselves together,
  as the manner of some is; but exhorting one another:
  and so much the more, as ye see the day approaching"
  (Hebrews 10:25).

- "Bless them which persecute you: bless, and curse not"
  (Romans 12:14).

- "Pray without ceasing" (1 Thessalonians 5:17).

Victory comes through obedience to the Word of God. When
you submit yourself to it, you will sense God's authority rest on

you, and you will observe his power in your life. You'll quit being stuck and start moving forward. This is the power of the Word in your life.

THE CREATIVE WORD: ACTIVATING THE SPIRIT

The fourth episode recorded in Luke 4 has to do with the creative power of the Word. When God speaks, it unleashes the power of the Spirit. We see that happening here at the launch of Jesus' public ministry. After Jesus cast the unclean spirit out of a man at the synagogue, the word quickly spread throughout the region. Later, Jesus healed Simon's mother-in-law of a high fever. By sunset, people from all over had come seeking healing. Jesus laid his hands on them and healed them. Some were demon possessed, and when the demons left them they shouted out Jesus' true identity, "Thou art Christ the Son of God" (Luke 4:41). Interestingly, this is the same affirmation Jesus received at his baptism; now it was obvious even to demons.

In this rapid expansion of Jesus' ministry, we see that the power of the Word—which had been affirmed at his baptism, exercised in his temptations, relied upon through rejection at Nazareth, and declared with authority at Capernaum—had unleashed the power of the Spirit. As a result, Jesus was healing people right and left and casting out demons in great number. The next day, Jesus set off on a ministry journey, saying, "I must preach the kingdom of God to other cities also: for therefore am I sent" (verse 43). Do you see what's happening? The Word, declared with authority, activated the work of the Spirit. It was like a precursor to the day of Pentecost. Jesus went out into the region to proclaim that same Word, the good news of the kingdom of God. Not surprisingly, miracles followed.

This pattern of the Word activating the Spirit is not something new. We see it first in Genesis 1, at the very beginning of the world. Everything was formless and empty, and dark. "And the Spirit of God moved upon the face of the waters" (Genesis 1:2). In the stillness, the Spirit was waiting. Then God spoke, "Let there be light" (verse 3). And what happened? There was light. The Word of God unleashed the creative power of the Spirit. The same will be true in your life when you know, apply, and declare the Word of God. God's Word activates the power of the Spirit.

Look at the power released through the ministry of Jesus. He commanded demons and they came out with a whimper, not hurting anyone (Luke 4:35). Jesus commanded illness to be gone, and it was gone (verse 39). Jesus healed with the touch of a hand (verse 40). He commanded demons not to speak, and they were silent (verse 41). All of this was possible because Jesus received his identity through the Word, applied it to his own life, and declared it with authority. When you exercise the Word in similar ways, you too will activate the power of the Spirit. You will be able to speak the good news with authority, and people will listen. You can declare the truth and rob the devil of his power. You will exercise your spiritual gift and see results in your life and ministry. You will see the barriers and obstacles that seem to hold you back in life begin to melt away as the Spirit works on your behalf. Think of the apostle Paul, who said, "I came to you . . . not with excellency of speech or of wisdom, declaring unto you the testimony of God. For I determined not to know any thing among you, save Jesus Christ, and him crucified. And I was with you in weakness, and in fear, and in much trembling. And my speech and my preaching was not with enticing words of man's wisdom, but in demonstration of the Spirit and of power" (1 Corinthians

2:1–4). Paul had no great talent or impressive characteristics. All he did was declare the Word with authority and it activated the Spirit's power.

Too many Christians chase after the Spirit as if by running from one church service or revival meeting to the next they could track him down and claim a blessing. In reality, the Spirit responds to the Word. Claim your identity through the Word. Know the Word and apply it to your life. Declare the Word with authority. That's when you'll see the Spirit begin to move in your life.

LIVING IN THE WORD

You are a whole person, having body, mind, and spirit. The point of knowing the Word is not to neglect your spirit. We simply want a balance between Word and Spirit, mind and heart, doctrine and emotion. Your heart does matter. You feel the joy of the Lord. You are moved to love others. You are roused to righteous anger by sin and injustice. All aspects of your person are important to God. However, if we have a particular weakness today it is that we overemphasize the spirit to the neglect of the mind. To correct that imbalance, you must apply yourself to knowing the Word and manifesting the Word in your life. Here are some practical things you can do to get the Word into your mind so it can produce results in your life.

Read the Bible. This may sound obvious, but it probably needs to be stated. The Word of God is a book, and we take it into our minds by reading. Reading is a struggle for some, but there are many free audio versions of the Bible available online. Make a goal to read the entire Bible. You don't have to do that all at once, but you'll never do it if you don't begin. With a solid plan, you can accomplish this in a year. Take longer if you wish. Just read consistently.

Study the Bible. Paul writes, "Study to shew thyself approved unto God, a workman that needeth not to be ashamed, rightly dividing the word of truth" (2 Timothy 2:15). You will gain greater insight into the Word by studying it, either on your own or in a group. If you are not in a Bible study, small group, or Sunday school class, join one. Bring your Bible to church and take notes on the sermon. Put forth some effort to acquire knowledge. It will pay off in power.

Memorize Scripture. The psalmist writes, "Thy word have I hid in mine heart, that I might not sin against thee" (Psalm 119:11). By committing portions of Scripture to memory, you make them readily available to aid you in times of temptation, discouragement, or adversity. This is easier than you may think. Simply take one verse at a time and repeat it daily until you have mastered it.

Meditate on Scripture. Take your interaction with the Word to a new level by meditating on it. This simply means to think it over, to let your mind dwell on it. The Spirit will reveal deeper insights to you as you allow the Word to wash over your mind throughout the day.

Affirm the Word. Cement your identity in the Word by daily affirming its truths. Choose biblical promises or statements of identity (such as those listed in this chapter) and say them aloud to yourself. Drill the Word into your mind by repeating its truths.

The term *doctrine* has fallen out of favor with some Christians. They think it implies an empty, purely intellectual faith that has no power. But doctrine is vitally important. Doctrines are the statements of truth, based on Scripture, that form our understanding of who God is and how he works. Without sound doctrine, we're like a little boat on the vast ocean, tossed this way and that by whatever winds of emotion or scraps of ideas blow our way. The simple solution is to base your life upon the Word. Allow the Word of God to form your identity, inform your decisions, and activate the Spirit's power in your life. Then, gradually, "precept upon precept; line upon line . . . here a little, and there a little" (Isaiah 28:10), you will go from stuck in place to stepping forward in victory. The Word will empower you to win.

THE SUCCESSFUL SEVEN

- Does your faith tend more to *mind* or *emotion*? Name one thing you can do to create balance in this area.

- If you do not own a Bible, get a copy in a version that is easy for you to read and understand. If you do own a Bible, consider adding a Bible app to your computer, phone, or tablet.

- List the biblical promises or affirmations that form your identity (such as those listed in this chapter). Place the list where you will see it every day.

- Name the three most powerful temptations that you face, and list biblical responses to those challenges.

- Make a specific plan to join a Bible study group. Which group will you join? When?

- From BibleGateway.com or YouVerson.com, choose a Bible reading plan and begin daily Bible reading.

- Memorize 2 Timothy 2:15.

PART 2
The Principles of Deliverance

This section will help you understand how God works in your life—even through the adversity you face—to bring about your deliverance. You will discover key biblical principles for growth by looking at the ways God dealt with his people in the Old Testament. These are key principles:

My present prepares me for God's future.

I don't have to wait to be free.

I must put myself in a position to win.

God works through my weaknesses, not my strengths.

As you apply this learning to your life, you will grow spiritually despite what you suffer, and you will prepare yourself for victory.

◇

5

Embrace the Hope of Our Promised Future

I am the Lord, *and I will bring you out from under
the burdens of the Egyptians, and I will rid you out of their
bondage, and I will redeem you with a stretched out arm,
and with great judgments.*
—Exodus 6:6

THE WINNING CONCEPT

My present prepares me for God's future.

LIFE IN THE JUNGLE

Sometimes good news is hard to accept. When you have
suffered a long time, pain becomes a constant companion.
Adversity can become a lifestyle. Though it may be uncomfort-
able, it is at least familiar. You may long for change, yet when
it finally comes the news may be difficult to accept. Such was

the experience of Lieutenant Hiroo Onoda of the Imperial Japanese Army. On December 26, 1944, during the waning days of
World War II, Lieutenant Onoda was called to meet with superior officers in Manila, the Philippines. His orders were to deploy
to Lubang, a small island some ninety-three miles southwest of
Manila, and lead a band of soldiers in disrupting the advance of
the American military. The war was not going well for the Japanese, and Onoda and his men would be more or less isolated on
the small island. Yet his commander gave him this promise: "It
may take three years, it may take five, but whatever happens, we'll
come back for you. Until then, so long as you have one soldier,
you are to continue to lead him. You may have to live on coconuts. If that's the case, live on coconuts! Under no circumstances
are you to give up your life voluntarily."

"*Yes, Sir!*" Onoda responded.[16]

The twenty-two-year-old lieutenant had joined the army in
1942 and trained as an intelligence officer. He had studied guer-
rilla warfare, philosophy, history, martial arts, propaganda, and
covert operations.[17] At last, he would have his opportunity to
serve the Emperor in combat. Within days he was deployed to
Lubang.

The momentum of the American forces was too great to be
stopped however, and they landed in the Philippines on February
28, 1945. Onoda and his men withdrew to the interior of the
small island of Lubang, intending to continue guerilla operations.
But within six months, the Japanese surrendered unconditionally
by order of the Emperor. World War II was officially over.

But not for Onoda. Having no radio contact with Tokyo,
he and his men had no idea that his country had been defeated,

---

16. Hiroo Onoda, *No Surrender: My Thirty-Year War* (Annapolis, MD: Naval Institute Press, 1974), 44.
17. Robert D. McFadden, "Hiroo Onoda, Soldier Who Hid in Jungle for Decades, Dies at 91," New York Times, January 17, 2014, https://www.nytimes.com/2014/01/18/world/asia/hiroo-onoda-imperial-japanese-army-officer-dies-at-91.html.

so they fought on. For one year, then another, they lived in the jungle, carrying out sporadic raids against the villages of Lubang. Five years went by, then ten. Onoda's men were gradually killed or captured. Meanwhile, the intrepid lieutenant continued living in the wilderness, patching his tattered uniform, foraging for food, and fighting alone, an army of one man against the world.

It wasn't that Onoda had no opportunity to learn the truth and trade his harsh, solitary existence for a return to his homeland. Over the years, many attempts had been made to contact the Japanese holdouts, including dropping leaflets from the air, broadcasting the good news by loudspeaker, and sending foot patrols to seek contact. Onoda had ignored them all. He simply refused to believe the truth.

Finally, the strange case of Lieutenant Onoda came to the attention of a Japanese adventurer named Norio Suzuki. In 1974, some thirty years after the war's end, Suzuki visited the island and was able to make contact with the holdout soldier, who was now nearly fifty-two years of age. At their first meeting, Suzuki advanced cautiously toward the old soldier.

"Are you Onoda-san?" Suzuki asked.

"Yes, I'm Onoda."

"Really, Lieutenant Onoda?"

The elder man nodded.

"I know you've had a long, hard time. The war's over. Won't you come back to Japan with me?"

But Onoda was unconvinced. He later recalled, "His use of polite Japanese expressions convinced me that he must have been brought up in Japan, but he was rushing things too much. Did he think he could just make the simple statement that the war was over and I would go running back to Japan with him? After all those years, it made me angry."

He told Suzuki, "No, I won't go back! For me, the war hasn't ended!"[18]

It took the return of Onoda's commanding officer, who was retired and living as a bookseller in Japan, to convince Lieutenant Onoda that the war had ended and that he could, at last, give up the fight and return to a normal life. The ragged soldier saluted and wept.[19]

Though it sounds strange to those who have not experienced it, some people prefer to live in adversity. After a time, suffering clouds their thinking and they can no longer conceive of a better life. The familiar pain of a toxic friendship, or living with a mountain of debt seems somehow preferable to the challenge of creating change. If you are to win over adversity, you must first win this battle in your own mind. You must break free from the negative thoughts that keep you bound in suffering and accept the good news, which is this: Your present suffering is merely a prelude to a glorious future. Your present prepares you for God's purpose.

HEARING PROBLEMS

If you have difficulty seeing God's purpose in your current circumstances, you are not alone. The Israelites had the same problem when Moses announced God's plan to bring them out of slavery. We read about that in Exodus 6. After God had told Moses all that he planned to do, Moses went and reported that good news to the people. "But they did not listen to him because of their discouragement and harsh labor" (Exodus 6:9). Like Lieutenant Onoda, the people had been living so long in exile that

18. Onoda, *No Surrender*, 198.
19. McFadden, "Hiroo Onoda."

they simply couldn't accept what they were hearing. They were beaten down and exhausted from their toil.

Several factors no doubt contributed to this inability to accept freedom. For one, the people had been living in slavery for some four hundred years. For comparison, think about what life was like in the early seventeenth century, about four hundred years before today. The King James Bible had not yet been created. The United States of America did not exist, only a smattering of Dutch, Spanish, French, and English settlements. William Shakespeare was still living. The Ming dynasty ruled China. Now imagine that you and your people have been slaves from then until now. What would your mindset be like? Could you even imagine that life could be different?

Also, this spiral into pessimism had come on gradually. After the glory days when Joseph was second in command in Egypt, reporting only to Pharaoh himself, a new leader came onto the scene, a Pharaoh who did not know Joseph or care much for the Hebrew people. Over time, the people were first forgotten, then feared, and finally oppressed. Slavery became normal to them. It was all they knew. No wonder they had difficulty accepting the grand vision that Moses laid out for them.

There may be many factors that prevent you from hearing the good news that your present suffering is merely preparation for God's glorious future. To accept that idea, you'll have to become aware of those factors and separate them from your thinking. Here are a few of the reasons it can be difficult to hear good news from the Lord. They are like background noise in a crowded restaurant. Remove these distractions and you'll be able to hear God's voice more clearly.

ADVERSITY SEEMS NORMAL

After four centuries in slavery, bondage seemed normal to the Hebrew people. It had become part of their identity. Sadly, that's a common effect of suffering. It makes the sufferer adopt a new perspective on life. When you suffer rejection by a spouse or loved one, you don't simply feel hurt. You conclude, "I'm unlovable," or, "There must be something wrong with me." When you are fired from a job, you may begin to think, "Nobody wants me. I have nothing to offer." When you fail in business or some other venture, you may globalize that failure, thinking, "I can't do anything right. I must be a loser."

Stop! None of those things are true. To see the future God has for you, you must be able to separate your current reality (the trouble you're in) from your core identity (who you are in Christ). Adversity is not your new normal. You are not doomed to a lifetime of struggle. The fact that you now face rejection, loss, grief, or poverty does not mean that you always will. Don't accept your negative circumstances as permanent. Whether they have lasted for a day or a decade, they don't have to last forever.

PAIN CLOUDS YOUR JUDGMENT

The Hebrew people couldn't accept the good news Moses brought them because of their discouragement. It's one thing to see your team lose a football game and to become pessimistic about their prospects for the season. The discouragement the Hebrew people faced was something else, something deeper. It was a pessimism born of year upon year of suffering. It was a complete inability to adopt a positive viewpoint. It was an entirely negative way of thinking, void of hope. Long-term suffering has a way of clouding our judgment so that we simply can't think in positive terms. That effect can go well beyond pessimism to cause those who suffer to make terrible mistakes in judgment, including harming themselves or others. They can't think rationally because of the pain they suffer—and that pain may be physical or emotional.

To put yourself in a position to hear from God, you must anchor yourself in positive thinking. Test your thoughts against Scripture and against the judgment of trusted friends. When you realize that your thinking is clouded, rely on the judgment of others. My friend Heather tells of a time, following a terrible tragedy in her life, when she was on the verge of losing her faith. A friend told her, "I will believe the promises of God for you, even if you can't believe them for yourself." Latching onto a friend's optimism pulled Heather through her time of adversity.

YOU'RE CONSTANTLY OVERWHELMED

Nearly everyone feels overwhelmed from time to time. When life gets too busy, you lack the time to eat properly, get enough rest, or think clearly about complex issues. Usually that lasts only for a season. But for some, being overwhelmed becomes a way of life. If you suffer from chronic pain, or are living in poverty, every day is a struggle. The daily business of earning a living, raising children, and managing your life is so overwhelming that you barely have time to think. All you can do is put one foot in front of the other.

To see clearly, you must create some space for yourself. Before you think about how to solve your problems, get some space from them so your mind can relax and your spirit can be refreshed. That's not always easy. You may have to fight for time alone, time without having to care for small children, time away from work.

Ask for help from family and friends. Practice the Sabbath discipline of rest. Get some respite from your situation so that you can calm your spirit, spend time in prayer, and listen to the voice of God.

YOU'RE DEPRESSED

Everyone feels sad from time to time, especially when they face difficulty. Nobody expects you to be chipper when you're ill, when a loved one dies, or when your basement is flooded. It's perfectly normal to feel negative emotions about negative events. But depression is something different. It is a psychological condition that affects mood, energy level, and judgment. People who suffer from depression have a difficult time seeing any positive future for themselves, even when things are changing for the better. They feel miserable and sad all the time.

When you feel that way, try the simplest solutions first. When King David faced a crushing defeat, we read that he "was greatly distressed; for the people spake of stoning him, because the soul of all the people was grieved, every man for his sons and for his daughters: but David encouraged himself in the LORD his God" (1 Samuel 30:6). David was able to rally his spirits by reminding himself of his relationship with God and of the Lord's promises to him. When you feel low, pray, affirm Bible truth, and call out to the Lord for help. That may be all you need.

However, don't be afraid to try other solutions as well. Call on friends to pray with you and encourage you. Look to your health, including proper rest, diet, and exercise. Seek out godly people to pray for your healing, and consult a doctor if need be. The Lord heals in many ways, and he may heal your depression through the intervention of a physician. If you are not able to hear from the

Lord or accept good news because of your mental state, then address that problem. Your outlook may be entirely different when you are able to change your mood.

God spoke his word to the Hebrew people through Moses, but they could not accept that word because of their discouragement and the harsh labor that was forced upon them. You may be experiencing the same thing. Before you can move forward into God's purpose for your life, you must be able to see through your problems to the blessing that waits on the other side. Remove the background noise of doubt and discouragement. Then you'll be able to hear the good news that God is preparing something better for you.

HEARING AIDS

Removing the background chatter is a step toward hearing God's voice more clearly. But even then, you may need some additional help. A hearing aid amplifies the good sound so a person who is hearing impaired can hear voices more clearly. When Moses began to address the people, he gave them a couple of hearing aids—positive reasons to receive the Word he proclaimed. These same principles can aid your hearing as well.

THIS WORD IS FROM GOD

Little words often have big meanings, and that's true of the tiny word *so* in Exodus 6:9. "And Moses spake so unto the children of Israel." That monosyllable tells us that Moses did not invent the message he delivered to the people. He was simply repeating the message that had been given to him by the Lord. That's true, or should be, of any prophet or preacher. We are not inventors of the divine Word; we are echoes of it. We're simply reflecting the

Word that has been passed on to us. The message that Moses delivered was the Word of God, and it was a message of freedom. He declared salvation from a cruel bondage, he declared hope, a glorious promise. This was the gospel—the good news—indeed. The message begins with the Word spoken to Moses in Exodus 6:2–5. When you remember these truths, you'll be better able to look beyond your problems and see the future.

> *And God spake unto Moses, and said unto him, I am the LORD: And I appeared unto Abraham, unto Isaac, and unto Jacob, by the name of God Almighty, but by my name JEHOVAH was I not known to them. And I have also established my covenant with them, to give them the land of Canaan, the land of their pilgrimage, wherein they were strangers. And I have also heard the groaning of the children of Israel, whom the Egyptians keep in bondage; and I have remembered my covenant. (Exodus 6:2–5)*

GOD IS IN CONTROL

The next thing we notice is that Moses began his message about the future by speaking about the past—he spoke to them about the God of Abraham, Isaac, and Jacob (verse 3). Moses recalled the days when God revealed himself to the patriarchs, the forefathers of the Israelites. God was not beginning a new thing. He was continuing the work that he had started long ago. Not only did God know that the Israelites were in slavery in Egypt, but he also had foretold that this would occur (see Genesis 15:13). God intended to use this adversity to refine the faith of his people.

Their suffering in Egypt was merely a prelude to the greater work of God in their lives.

The same is true for you. All the days of your life are numbered, and God knows each one. What you are suffering now is not hidden from him. And the deliverance that he will bring for you is not a new plan, as if God were starting from scratch. He will use this present adversity in a way that builds your faith and brings him glory. God is in control now, just as he has always been. Worship, after all, is a time of remembering what God has already done. The Passover was created so that the people would remember their deliverance from slavery. When Jesus instituted the Lord's Supper, he did so with the words, "This do in remembrance of me" (Luke 22:19). Remember what God has done. It will help you see and hear what he will do in the future.

GOD'S PROMISES ARE SECURE

Another lesson in this message to the Israelites is that it concerns the covenant (Exodus 6:4). Moses reminded the people that they had a powerful God who had first appeared to their forefathers centuries ago and had made a deal with them that included certain promises. One of the promises was that the descendants of Abraham would inherit the land of Canaan (see Genesis 6:7). For people living in slavery, that may have been hard to remember. Yet it was true. The promises God had given to Abraham, Isaac, and Jacob were still in effect.

When life is overwhelming for you, remember the promises that God has made. They are still good, and when you remember them it will be easier to hear the word God is speaking to you now. God has promised a hope and a future (Jeremiah 29:11), provision for our daily needs (Matthew 6:31–34), healing (James

5:15), escape from temptation (1 Corinthians 10:13), protection (Psalm 91:4–6), and many more good things. Most important, God has made a covenant promise that you will inherit eternal life through faith in Jesus Christ (1 John 2:25). Remember that, and it will aid you in hearing God's specific vision for your future.

GOD LOVES YOU

Next, we notice that Moses spoke to the people about God's mercy. God said that he had heard the groaning of the children of Israel (Exodus 6:5). He had compassion on them. He cared for them, and he had come to their rescue. Mercy is part of God's character. He is a God who loves deeply and acts mercifully.

Love is central to who God is, as the apostle John reminds us, "God is love" (1 John 4:8). Showing mercy comes naturally to him. He's wired for compassion. He loves people, and he loves you. When you feel overwhelmed by suffering, unable to think about the future, remember this central fact: God loves you. That may be hard to hear at times, meaning that you can hardly believe it because life hurts so much. Yet when you can accept that truth, it will become your best hearing aid, enabling you to accept God's plan and purpose for your life.

Now that you are in a better position to hear the Word of the Lord, let's take a look at the remainder of the message that Moses delivered to the Hebrew people. This positive message comes in five parts, and we'll see how each part bears on your present—and your future. Together, they reinforce the idea that our suffering is only temporary, a mere preparation for our future blessing.

THE FIVE DIMENSIONS OF BLESSING

Moses' message to the children of Israel was good news. He spoke a message of freedom and that message goes for you too.

The Israelites were our forerunners. Their slavery in Egypt is a parallel to our slavery to sin. Their release from captivity is a harbinger of our release from bondage. Their victory is our victory. So, the Word of God they received is the Word of God for you too. It is a word of salvation, hope, and promise.

For many centuries, commentators pointed out four statements in this message, found in Exodus 6:6–7, that identify four dimensions of salvation. In the Passover meal, each statement was tied to one of the four cups of wine taken with the meal. The psalms make a nice backdrop for this practice, as the psalmist writes, "I will take the cup of salvation, and call upon the name of the LORD" (Psalm 116:13). Later, the great Jewish scholar and philosopher Maimonides, who lived in the twelfth century, identified a fifth dimension of salvation in verse 8.

Let's look at the five dimensions of blessing promised to God's people, symbolized by five cups of salvation. Through them, you will begin to see the positive future God has in store for you. This is the good news that your present is merely a prelude to God's purpose in your life.

> *Wherefore say unto the children of Israel, I am the LORD, and I will bring you out from under the burdens of the Egyptians, and I will rid you out of their bondage, and I will redeem you with a stretched out arm, and with great judgments: And I will take you to me for a people, and I will be to you a God: and ye shall know that I am the LORD your God, which bringeth you out from under the burdens of the Egyptians. And I will bring you in unto the land, concerning the which I did swear*

to give it to Abraham, to Isaac, and to Jacob; and
I will give it you for an heritage: I am the LORD.
(Exodus 6:6–8)

THE FIRST DIMENSION: SANCTIFICATION

The first cup of blessing represents *sanctification,* based on the statement "I am the LORD, and I will bring you out from under the burdens of the Egyptians" (verse 6). This signifies that the people were chosen by God and set apart for his purpose. As slaves of the Egyptians, the Israelites could not worship God as he had instructed. Israel was intended to be a holy people, set apart for God alone. In fact, that is a primary meaning of the word *holy* or *sanctified.* Something that is holy is set apart for God. Living under the thumb of the Egyptians, they could never be that. They would always have to follow the dictates of their masters. So, the first blessing of salvation is that the people would be free *for* a relationship with God. Remember, when Moses told Pharaoh to release the people, it was so that they could go into the desert and worship (Exodus 5:1). God wanted people whose lives were set apart for him. He still does.

The first blessing of salvation for you, regardless of your current circumstances, is sanctification. You are chosen by God and set apart for him. Your life has a purpose. You have been freed from the guilt of sin so that you can worship the Lord with a clear conscience. You have been freed from the power of sin so that you can serve God with your whole heart. When you are mired in problems, adversity, or suffering, it is difficult to remember that you are called to be holy—set apart for God's glory. But that's exactly what you are. God told the prophet Jeremiah, "Before I formed thee in the belly I knew thee; and before thou camest forth out of the womb I sanctified thee, and I ordained thee a prophet unto the nations" (Jeremiah 1:5). The same is true for you. God has a purpose in mind for your life. You are set apart for him. Whatever you face right now, it's not final. God has set you apart for something better.

THE SECOND DIMENSION: DELIVERANCE

The second cup of blessing represents *deliverance*, based on the statement, "I will rid you out of their bondage" (Exodus 6:6). This reminded the people that they would not only be free *for* God's purpose, they would also be free *from* the bondage of their oppressors. Israel was helpless in their predicament as slaves. They had no power to change their situation. But God could liberate them, and he did. He delivered them from the power of the mightiest nation on earth at that time, and he did so despite the military action of Pharaoh and his army. The situation was grave, but God was greater.

Your current circumstances may have you feeling powerless also. You may be mired in temptation, unable to free yourself from a besetting sin that has conquered you time after time. You may feel helpless because of the actions of others, such as a boss or teacher or family member. Perhaps you feel trapped in credit card debt or other financial needs. Here's the good news: God is greater. Whatever your problems may be, God has the power to deliver you from them. That doesn't mean the process will be simple or instantaneous. Remember that the Israelites had to learn to trust God in the desert, a process that took forty years. The timetable is less important than the Timekeeper. God has the ability to deliver you from sin, from debt, from oppression, from illness, from adversity, and he will do it in his time and in his way. He will break the yoke of Satan from your neck and make you no more the slave of sin. You shall be a child of the living God, set apart to serve him with your whole heart.

THE THIRD DIMENSION: REDEMPTION

The third cup of blessing represents *redemption*, based on the statement, "I will redeem you with a stretched out arm" (Exodus 6:6). In the Passover celebration, this cup symbolizes the blood of the Passover lamb. When God delivered the people from slavery, he won a spiritual victory as well as a military one. For God defeated not only Pharaoh and the forces of Egypt but also death and the powers of darkness. Remember that without the shedding of blood, there is no remission of sin (Hebrews 9:22). There was a price for Israel's redemption, and God paid that price.

We know, of course, that the Passover lamb was a symbol for Christ, our eternal sacrifice. When Jesus instituted the Lord's Supper, he said, "This cup is the new covenant in my blood, which is poured out for you" (Luke 22:20 NIV). Our salvation was purchased by our Lord's sacrifice on the cross. Christ is our redeemer. He has brought us back from death to life. Jesus' blood did not merely cover our sin; it washed that sin away.

Christ has redeemed you, which means that you have a new future. He did this at great cost to himself, the sacrifice of his own life. Therefore, your life has great value. When you are suffering from rejection, failure, defeat, loneliness, or grief, the world doesn't seem to make sense. Your own life seems to be pointless. "What's the use?" you may ask yourself. But remember that God places infinite value on your life, regardless of your current circumstance and despite your past failures. God values you! When you realize that, it becomes obvious that your present adversity cannot define your life. There is something beyond this, something more that God has in store for you.

THE FOURTH DIMENSION: RESTORATION

The fourth cup of blessing represents *restoration,* based on the statement, "I will take you to me for a people, and I will be to you a God" (Exodus 6:7). The Israelites had lost something. They had lost their former way of life. They had lost the close communication with God that Abraham, Isaac, and Jacob had enjoyed. Their slavery had robbed them of this blessing. Through this fourth cup, Moses reminded the people that what had been lost would be restored. God would once again draw near to the Israelites. The blessing of fellowship with God would be restored.

Adversity of any kind is a thief, robbing us of hope, joy, peace, purpose, and fellowship. When you face a particular hardship, whether it is physical, emotional, relational, or financial, you may think longingly about the way things used to be. You recall the days when you didn't have to worry about money. You remember the way it was before you had troubles in your marriage, when you both felt deeply in love. You think longingly of the time when your body was free from pain and you could move freely, go where you chose to go, and had energy to do the things that you wanted to do. This fourth cup reminds us that God will restore our fortunes. As God promised through the prophet Joel, "And I will restore to you the years that the locust hath eaten" (Joel 2:25).

We have confidence that God will bring restoration. Yet we must beware of taking this as a promise of recreating life exactly as it was, in every detail. For example, if you have lost your job, restoration does not mean getting your exact same job back. It means that God promises to provide for your needs so that you can be secure in him. When you are stuck in a rut, it's hard to imagine life any other way. The cup of restoration reminds us that God can restore us to the blessings we once enjoyed—and even more.

THE FIFTH DIMENSION: HOPE

The fifth cup of blessing signifies *hope,* based on the statement, "I will bring you in unto the land" (Exodus 6:8). This cup reminds us that a part of our blessing is yet to be realized. When the Israelites crossed the Red Sea, they were delivered from slavery in Egypt. They were free to worship and serve God. They had been restored to fellowship with him. But they were not yet in the Promised Land. They still had a long way to go. This cup was a reminder that God would in fact bring them into that land, just as he had promised. This cup represents hope for the future.

For you, fighting to overcome adversity and struggling to claim your freedom and move forward in faith, may well be the most important dimension of salvation. We all need hope. Having made the decision to live as an overcomer, you may be disappointed at the pace of change in your life. You expect deliverance to be immediate, but it may take time, just as it did for the Israelites. Have you never noticed that when you take medicine, you sometimes feel worse before you start to get better? It helps to hear the doctor's reassurance, "It will work. Just give it time." Drink deeply from this fifth cup of blessing. Imbibe the powerful medicine of hope. Let it course through your veins and stimulate your mind. What you see right now, your current circumstances, are far from final. Your present is a mere prologue, preparing you for God's purpose. Don't lose hope.

CUBS WIN!

You don't have to be much of a baseball fan to know the dismal history of the Chicago Cubs. This historic team was founded in 1870 and was very strong in the early twentieth century, winning back-to-back World Series in 1907 and 1908. Yet over the next century and more, the Cubs lost far more games than they won. Though they made it to the World Series in seven additional seasons, they lost every time. After more than a hundred years of losing, barely a person alive had ever known the Cubs as champions. Their fans became known for their dour patience. They were a little melancholy, perhaps, but always hopeful that next year could be their year.

Then came the 2016 season. More than a century after their last championship, the Cubs defeated the Cleveland Indians four games to three, claiming the greatest prize in Major League Baseball, the World Series Championship. After 108 long years, elated fans could scream at the top of their lungs, "Cubs win!" The victory was all the sweeter because their fans never lost hope. They did not allow their experience ("We always lose") to shape their future vision ("We can win!").

Take a lesson from those longsuffering baseball fans. Do not become so discouraged by your circumstances that you cannot envision a better future. Do not allow your current reality to define your purpose. God loves you. He has redeemed you. He will deliver you. Your present suffering is a preparation for God's glorious future. Hear this good news.

THE SUCCESSFUL SEVEN

- List the things that make it difficult to believe your life can change, then state a biblical promise in response to each one.

- Name one practical action you can take to gain a fresh perspective on your problems.

- Name one person you can talk to about your most overwhelming problem, then make an appointment to speak with that person.

- Each day for one week, pray and meditate on God's purpose for your life, then write a brief paragraph describing that purpose.

- List ten promises God has made in the Bible.

- Describe some ways that your current adversity may be strengthening or preparing you for the future.

- Memorize Exodus 6:6.

◇

6

The Blessing That Comes from Adversity

If you belong to Christ, then you are Abraham's seed,
and heirs according to the promise.
—Galatians 3:29 NIV

THE WINNING CONCEPT

I don't have to wait to be free.

WHEN PIGS FLY

Do you learn from your mistakes? I can assure you that US Airways does. Several years ago, boarding agents in Philadelphia allowed a three-hundred-pound Vietnamese potbellied pig named Charlotte to travel first class—*for free*—on a flight to Seattle, accompanying the pig's owner. The woman had told the airline that Charlotte was a therapeutic animal, similar to a guide dog.[20] However, witnesses reported that the pig became unruly

---

20. The Associated Press, "US Airways was right to allow pig on plane," *The Arizona Daily Wildcat Online,* November 30, 2000, http://wc.arizona.edu/papers/94/70/01_95_m.html.

at the end of the six-hour flight, and, as the jet taxied toward the Seattle terminal, started running through the plane squealing. "Many people on board the aircraft were quite upset that there was a large uncontrollable pig on board, especially those in the first-class cabin," the incident report stated.

"We can confirm that the pig traveled, and we can confirm that it will never happen again," said a US Airways spokesman. "Let me stress that. It will never happen again."[21]

Federal regulations do allow pigs to fly as service animals. In fact, if an airline employee determines that a pig, miniature horse, or even a monkey is a legitimate human helper and does not pose a threat to health, safety, or airline operations, they must permit it aboard.[22]

Even so, US Airways later stuck with its position and kicked a pig off a recent flight from Connecticut. One passenger reported that a woman boarded the flight carrying a duffel bag concealing a pig weighing fifty to seventy pounds. "We could smell it," he noted. Although the woman claimed the pig was an emotional support animal, she was asked to leave the plane before takeoff because the pig was disruptive.[23] She deplaned without ceremony, carrying the stinky swine over one shoulder.

That seems like a no-brainer, doesn't it? You might be fooled once by a good pig story, but you'd likely learn from your mistake. To operate a successful business—or to be successful in life—you must learn from the past. Experience is a great teacher, if we're willing to listen.

When it comes to living as an overcomer, you must be able to learn from the past in order to move into the future. You will

21. The Associated Press, "Pig Flies First Class Across U.S.," *The Washington Post* online edition, October 27, 2000, http://www.washingtonpost.com/wp-srv/aponline/20001027/aponline212651_000.htm.
22. Code of Federal Regulations, Title 14, Chapter II, Subchapter D, §382:117(f) "Must carriers permit passengers with a disability to travel with service animals?" U.S. Government Publishing Office, current as of January 20, 2017, http://www.ecfr.gov/cgi-bin/text-idx?SID=215f062a73d67d9db4c46ad2582dd3ac&mc=true&node=pt14.4.382&rgn=div5.
23. Rheana Murray, "Here's Proof Pigs Actually Do Fly (Almost)," ABC News website, November 27, 2014, http://abcnews.go.com/US/proof-pigs-fly/story?id=27222136.

never get unstuck if you keep spinning your wheels by making the same old mistakes and thinking the same old thoughts. God has a great future in store for you. He has promised great blessings that are yours to receive. And here's the really good part—those blessings are available to you right now! But in order to claim them, you must adopt a new mindset. You must prepare for the future by learning from the past. In this chapter you will see how a change of mindset will enable you to receive God's blessing, not someday, not far off in the distant future, but right now.

MOVING BEYOND THE PAST

To move beyond where you are and into the new place God has in store, you must deal with the errors that have kept you stuck for so long. Sometimes these are glaring mistakes and outright sins. At other times, they may be subtle, such as wrong ideas or unbiblical thinking. Moses understood this. By the end of his career, Moses had led the Israelites for forty years. Nearly all of that time had been spent wandering in the wilderness, where both Moses and the people made their share of mistakes. Moses had a bad temper and that caused him to act foolishly at times. The people were selfish, unruly, and often unwilling to follow the Lord's leading. Knowing that the end of his life was approaching, Moses gathered the people for a final blessing. They would soon realize the dream, entering the Promised Land. At last, they would get unstuck—moving out of the wilderness and into the Land of Milk and Honey. Yet Moses knew that if they were to claim that long-awaited blessing, they would have to be done with the sort of thinking that had kept them stuck in the past. So before pronouncing God's blessing on the people, Moses gave them a little history lesson. In it, Moses identified four lessons the people would need to embrace before they could move into the future.

These lessons apply to you too. As a child of God, you stand to inherit this same blessing Moses pronounced on the people. It is, in fact, the original blessing God had given to Adam, repeated and expanded for Abraham, and made available to all through Jesus Christ. To claim it, you must move beyond old ways of thinking and learn from the past—Israel's and yours.

LEARN FROM THE MISTAKES OF THE PAST

This occasion when Moses blessed the people is recorded in Deuteronomy 33. Deuteronomy means "second law." This is not another law, but it is a retelling of the laws that God had given the people through Moses. Review and repetition are always helpful for learning, but there's something else here to note. This time through, Moses also gave a history lesson. He recalled the history of the previous generations, mentioning each of the twelve tribes by name. These were the people who had heard the law the first time, beginning at Mount Sinai.

You may know a bit of their history. That older generation, the people who came out of slavery in Egypt, proved to be unfaithful at nearly every turn, culminating with their refusal to enter the Promised Land when God first directed them to do so. As they neared the land of Canaan, they sent twelve spies into the land, one from each tribe. The spies came back and reported that the land was truly abundant, but the people who lived there were too powerful to overcome. Only two of the twelve, Joshua and Caleb, recommended following God's plan and entering the land. Hearing the discouraging report from the majority of the spies, the people lost heart and refused to enter. As a result, God declared that not one person who had been led out of Egypt would enter the land, except for Joshua and Caleb. Not even Moses was allowed to enter. (You can read this story in Numbers 13–14.) Moses alluded to this history as a way of warning the people not to make the same mistakes again. They needed to learn from the past if they were to move into the future.

You must do the same. If you are to receive God's blessing in the future, you must be sure that you won't repeat the mistakes of your past. When were the times that you didn't trust God, preferring to remain stuck over the risk of following the Lord? Where are your weak spots, the places at which you are especially vulnerable to temptation? How have you failed the Lord, others, yourself? What have you learned from those mistakes? How will you guard against them in the future?

Moses was right to remind the people of their history, even though it was probably hard for them to hear. You must identify and correct the failures of the past if you hope to move into a better future.

ADOPT A NEW WAY OF THINKING

If you travel in the United Kingdom, you may see the words "Look Right" painted on the pavement near a crosswalk. It's a reminder that cross-traffic will be coming from the right. That can be helpful for anyone from countries where we drive on the opposite side of the road. We are used to looking to the left before stepping into the street. It would be a shame to die because you had a wrong idea stuck in your head. Sadly, that's exactly what happened to the first generation of Israelites.

That older generation all died in the wilderness because they had the wrong mindset. They had come from the bondage of

Egypt, and they could never quite get accustomed to thinking in terms of freedom. As soon as they faced the least hardship, they begged to go back to Egypt. When Moses took too long on Mount Sinai, receiving the law directly from God, the people gave up on him and tried to invent their own gods. They refused to believe that they, former slaves, could conquer the nations of Canaan. They could never break that old way of thinking. They allowed themselves to be defined by the process and not by the mission. They could see the struggle but not the victory. Moses knew that the present generation would have to "look right" if they were going to seize the Promised Land. They needed a new way of thinking.

You do too. If you're going to get unstuck, you must start thinking like an overcomer. Don't get so lost in the struggle that you can't envision victory. Are there ways in which you think like a slave? How often do you find yourself complaining, naysaying, or listing objections rather than voicing hope? Is your outlook characterized more by despair or by joy? Are you more afraid of moving into the future than of staying in your safe, comfortable mess?

God's blessings are available to his children, but only to those who will receive them. Think about the way you think. Do you focus more on the obstacles than on the goal? You must adopt the mindset of an overcomer before you can receive God's blessings.

ADOPT A NEW IDENTITY

The generation that died in the wilderness had a negative mindset, and at the root of their thinking was a mistaken self-identity. They saw themselves as weak and helpless, and that's just what they became. The report of the spies, who brought back that terrible report from Canaan, culminates with this statement: "And there we saw the giants, the sons of Anak, which come of the giants: and we were in our own sight as grasshoppers, and so we were in their sight" (Numbers 13:33). Did you catch that? They compared themselves to the people of the land, who looked like giants to them. And that made them feel small. So that's how they saw themselves, and that is how they acted, and that is how other people saw them too.

Feeling small is the inevitable result of comparing yourself to others. To think like an overcomer, you must stop comparing yourself to other people and pay attention to what God says about you. You are an overcomer (1 John 5:4), a new creation (2 Corinthians 5:17), and a conqueror (Romans 8:37). Identify yourself by your future, not by your past or your present. And whatever you do, do not identify yourself by the people around you. You will always be able to point to someone who is taller, smarter, braver, more optimistic, holier, or more devoted. At least that's how they will appear to you. Making such comparisons leaves you feeling deflated and stuck. The way you see yourself will largely determine how you see the world and how you view the challenges you face. Find your true identity in what God says about you. Let that positive, optimistic vision guide you into the future.

BE EMPOWERED

Moses was a great leader. Under God's direction, he led the people out of slavery, guided them through years in the wilderness, gave them the law, and formed them into a nation. Those are stellar achievements by any standard. Yet as great as Moses was, he could take the people no further. A new leader, Joshua, would have to take his place. The people would have to move forward without the man they had depended upon for so long. For the generation that would soon enter the Promised Land, Moses was the only leader they had ever known. One of Moses' aims in this transition was to inspire the people with courage. He wanted to empower them with the knowledge that they could succeed without him, if they would depend on God. To do so, he made this statement about taking on the enemies who lay just over the Jordan River: "Be strong and of a good courage, fear not, nor be afraid of them: for the LORD thy God, he it is that doth go with thee; he will not fail thee, nor forsake thee" (Deuteronomy 31:6). The fact that Moses had to tell the people to be strong shows that they felt just the opposite. They felt weak, helpless, unable to take on the challenge. They needed to be empowered. They would not conquer the Promised Land by wringing their hands.

You also must be empowered if you are to move forward. Feeling helpless keeps you stuck in place. To claim the blessing of God, you must rise up to it. You must see yourself as able, responsible, and capable of following God wherever he leads. That doesn't mean it will be easy. The road ahead will be difficult and sometimes daunting. But you must have courage. Someone has said that courage is not an absence of fear but a willingness to move forward in spite of fear. Where are the places in life where you tend to shrink back and avoid taking action? How often do you find yourself saying, "I can't"? Be strong; have courage. You have both the ability and the responsibility to take action in your situation. You can't do everything, but God can. He will do amazing things with those who trust him. Be one of those people.

THE NATURE OF BLESSING

Moses had prepared the people to receive God's blessing. It's likely that people in biblical times had a better understanding of what a blessing is than we do. A blessing is not simply a brief prayer before meals or a polite thing to say when someone sneezes. A blessing is a future already decided. It is a declaration of God's will, delivered while you are in a state both to believe it and to act upon it. A blessing is a gift from God, made available for you to receive by faith.

When you choose to win, you're making the decision to accept God's blessing on your life. You're saying, in effect, "No more sitting and waiting, no more feeling helpless, no more saying 'I can't.' I want all that God has in store for me." The Bible is filled with descriptions of God's blessings and we are about to review one of them, the blessing Moses pronounced upon the tribe of Asher. Before we review the details of that blessing, you must understand these three essential characteristics of a blessing.

BLESSINGS ARE IRREVOCABLE

A blessing is fixed; it cannot be altered because it is the Word of God. Once you are blessed, you are blessed. We see that principle illustrated in the passing of the Abrahamic blessing from Abraham's son Isaac, to Isaac's son, Jacob. The story is recorded in Genesis 27. Isaac had inherited God's blessing from Abraham, and at the end of his life he was to pass it on to his firstborn son, Esau. However, Isaac's younger son, Jacob, swindled his brother Esau out of his birthright. Jacob then tricked his father into pronouncing the blessing upon him rather than upon Esau. So, Isaac pronounced the blessing upon Jacob, thinking it was Esau whom he was blessing. Just then, Esau arrived on the scene and realized what had happened. Here's what followed: "And when Esau heard the words of his father, he cried with a great and exceeding bitter cry, and said unto his father, Bless me, even me also, O my father. And he said, Thy brother came with subtilty, and hath taken away thy blessing" (Genesis 27:34–35). Once given, the blessing could not be revoked, even though Isaac may have wished to do so. A blessing is irrevocable.

When God pronounced his blessing to Abraham, we read, "For when God made promise to Abraham, because he could swear by no greater, he sware by himself, Saying, Surely blessing I will bless thee, and multiplying I will multiply thee" (Hebrews 6:13–14). Note how emphatic that statement is. God swore by himself, saying that he will surely carry out his Word. God's Word cannot be broken. When God has pronounced a blessing, nothing can stand in its way. Remember that the blessing you seek has been pronounced by God and is immovable. It is promised, and that promise is secure.

BLESSINGS BECOME GREATER WITH TIME

When God created the world, he pronounced a blessing on the first human pair, Adam and Eve. "God blessed them, and God said unto them, Be fruitful, and multiply, and replenish the earth, and subdue it: and have dominion over the fish of the sea, and over the fowl of the air, and over every living thing that moveth upon the earth" (Genesis 1:28). This was a blessing of abundance, dominion, and multiplication. Unfortunately, Adam and Eve failed to grasp that blessing because of their sin, instead invoking God's curse. The blessing, however, did not go away. It was later repeated and expanded when given to Abraham.

God said to Abraham, "I will make of thee a great nation, and I will bless thee, and make thy name great; and thou shalt be a blessing: And I will bless them that bless thee, and curse him that curseth thee: and in thee shall all families of the earth be blessed" (Genesis 12:2–3), and, "Thou shalt be a father of many nations. . . And I will make thee exceeding fruitful, and I will make nations of thee, and kings shall come out of thee. . . And I will give unto thee, and to thy seed after thee, the land wherein thou art a stranger, all the land of Canaan, for an everlasting possession; and I will be their God" (Genesis 17:4–8). Notice that in addition to abundance, dominion, and multiplication, God added that Abraham would in turn bless the world. The blessing was enlarged.

This blessing that God pronounced first to Adam, then to Abraham, was expanded again through Christ to include freedom from sin. The writer of Hebrews states God's promise this way: "I will make a new covenant with the house of Israel and with the house of Judah . . . For I will be merciful to their unrighteousness, and their sins and their iniquities will I remember no more" (Hebrews 8:8, 12). This new covenant makes available the blessings of fellowship with God (Hebrews 8:10) and eternal life (Romans 6:23). All that God had promised remains available, and to those promises were added others. As Hebrews puts it, "The new covenant is established on better promises" (Hebrews 8:6 NIV). What God began with Adam and continued with Abraham is still coming to pass.

BLESSINGS ARE AVAILABLE TO YOU

According to Scripture, the blessings that began with Adam and were expanded when given to Abraham and again through Christ are available to you right now. These blessings were first given to Adam, then repeated to Abraham. So how is it that we can claim them? To answer that question, we must remember two important points in Scripture. First, the apostle Paul states that Christ is the new Adam. "And so it is written, The first man Adam was made a living soul; the last Adam was made a quickening spirit" (1 Corinthians 15:45). This time, "Adam" brings life, not death. Through Christ, we are heirs to all that God promised Adam and more.

Second, Paul stated that the descendants of Abraham are not just the literal offspring of Abraham, Isaac, and Jacob—that is, not just the Jewish people. For by faith in Christ, *all* who believe are Abraham's children. Paul writes: "Understand, then, that those who have faith are children of Abraham. Scripture foresaw that God would justify the Gentiles by faith, and announced the gospel in advance to Abraham: 'All nations will be blessed through you.' So those who rely on faith are blessed along with Abraham, the man of faith" (Galatians 3:7–9 NIV).

So what's the result? "If you belong to Christ, then you are Abraham's seed, and heirs according to the promise" (Galatians 3:29 NIV). Translation: All of the promises God made to Abraham belong to you too. If you have faith in Christ and if you, like the Israelites whom Moses blessed, are willing to learn from the past, claim your true identity, and move forward in faith, you can claim that blessing right now. The only thing standing between you and all the blessings of God is your willingness to trust God and act in faith.

Let that sink in for a minute. That news may sound too good to be true, and like the Hebrew slaves, you may be struggling to rise above your discouragement and accept it. But you can trust the promises of God. They are irrevocable. Let's now examine the blessing that Moses pronounced on the Israelites just before they entered the Promised Land. As we've seen, this blessing is yours too, if you have the faith to accept it. Let's find out what it means.

STEPPING INTO THE NEW REALITY

Here's something interesting. When Moses stood to address the people for what would be his final speech, he was referred to as a king. "And he was king in Jeshurun, when the heads of the people and the tribes of Israel were gathered together" (Deuteronomy 33:5). The name *Jeshurun* means "upright one" and is a poetic name for Israel used in the Bible. Though Israel had no king and would have none for many years to come, Moses was declared king so he could usher in the age of a new kingdom. This was a pivotal point in the history of Israel. They were moving from stuck (wandering in the wilderness) to blessed (entering the Promised Land). Moses ushered in that new reality by invoking a blessing upon the people.

Here's another interesting fact. Moses did not bless the twelve tribes in the order of their birth—that is, in the order of the birth of their patriarch. That would have been the usual way to offer a blessing, going in birth order. Why did Moses change the order? It wasn't that he forgot or was confused. He did so as a prophetic statement. Moses began with Reuben, who was the firstborn, but he offered only a brief blessing upon that tribe. From there he mixed the order and ended with Asher, whose name means "blessed." Moses pronounced a lengthy and generous blessing on this eighth tribe. By varying the order of the tribes, Moses was creating a new reality. He called the people to step into a new age of God's blessing. Let's take a look at the five parts of this pronouncement and see the blessing that is available to you today.

1. THE BLESSING OF ABUNDANCE

The first blessing pronounced on Asher is the blessing of *abundance*. Moses declared, "Let Asher be blessed with children" (Deuteronomy 33:24). The blessing of children was especially meaningful in biblical times when families depended on their offspring for agricultural work and to care for them in their old age. The birth of Asher himself represented the end of a struggle to bring forth children. The blessing of children symbolizes the abundant harvest. So this blessing, that Asher would be blessed with children, is a blessing of ample provision. Asher was to be blessed with abundance.

That this blessing is available today should be beyond dispute. Jesus himself promised that God will provide our food and clothing (Matthew 6:25–26), and Paul writes, "My God shall supply all your need according to his riches in glory by Christ Jesus" (Philippians 4:19). From Elijah's multiplication of the widow's oil, to the feeding of the five thousand, to the miraculous catch of fish, the Bible is replete with stories designed to show the blessing of abundance. God will provide for his children not at a subsistence level only, but in abundance.

Why then do we not experience this blessing? One reason is because we approach life with a scarcity mindset, as if there were barely enough food in God's cupboard to go around. We hoard our goods rather than sharing them, believing that the twenty dollars in our pocket may be the last that God will provide. We refuse to share with the needy. We withhold our tithes and offerings. We treat everything from food to housing to good ideas as if we'll never see another come along. Remember that we are blessed to be a blessing. When we freely give, we freely receive. To step into the blessing of abundance, you must get beyond the scarcity thinking that has kept you a beggar for so long and begin to trust God. Adopt an abundance mentality and you will begin to see the full measure of God's provision.

2. THE BLESSING OF FAVOR

The second blessing pronounced on Asher is the blessing of *favor*. Moses declared, "Let him be acceptable to his brethren" (Deuteronomy 33:24). The role of the tribe of Asher was to produce oil for the sanctuary. This service was a benefit to all of Israel. Because of this selfless provision, Asher would enjoy the favor of other tribes. The people of Asher weren't simply looking out for themselves; they helped move the whole kingdom forward. They taught their daughters to marry into the priesthood, ignoring the risk to their own tribe's identity. As a result, they were favored by their neighbors.

Favor is a wonderful blessing because it opens up many possibilities. Joseph enjoyed the favor of Pharaoh, and he was able to bless not only his own family but also the entire nation of Egypt. King David enjoyed the favor of the people, and he was able to lead them to great victories over Israel's enemies. When you have favor, you have opportunity and possibility.

Many Christians today have difficulty claiming this blessing. It might be said that the church as a whole has struggled to find favor in our society. Rather than being blessed by others and finding unlimited opportunity, we often seem to be fighting battles with one another and with those around us. One reason is that we are rooted in a mindset of conflict. We view one another as competitors rather than comrades. We are jealous of our own reputation and achievements rather than thinking of the needs of others first. When you begin to bless others, you will begin to enjoy the blessing of favor. When you can put aside the petty feelings that drive you to put yourself first, when you can be genuinely interested in the welfare of others, even of nonbelievers, when you can adopt the mindset of a giver and not a taker, then you will know the blessing of favor.

3. THE BLESSING OF WEALTH

The third blessing pronounced on Asher is the blessing of *wealth*. Moses declared, "And let him dip his foot in oil" (Deuteronomy 33:24). Oil was a valuable commodity in biblical times, as it is today. Because Asher produced oil for the temple and the benefit of the priests, God blessed them with an abundance of oil—so much so that they could bathe their feet in it. Think of Mary, the sister of Lazarus, anointing Jesus' feet with pure nard (Matthew 26:6–13). What an extravagant act! Asher was blessed with oil to spare.

Once again, we see this blessing tied to obedience. Asher provided oil for the sanctuary, and they were granted an abundance of oil as a result. They were not given oil to hoard or to spend on themselves. Their wealth had a purpose: to bless others.

Jesus promised this blessing too. "Give, and it shall be given unto you; good measure, pressed down, and shaken together, and running over, shall men give into your bosom. For with the same measure that ye mete withal it shall be measured to you again" (Luke 6:38). Notice that here also the blessing is tied to obedience. When you freely give, you freely receive. The level of your generosity toward others will be the level of God's blessing in your life. How much wealth do you want to receive? How much are you willing to give away?

The reason we don't see greater prosperity in our lives is because we are stuck in a poverty mentality. Similar to abundance of food or material goods, the multiplying of wealth is directly tied to our mindset. When we are willing to invest in the kingdom, be generous with others, help the poor, and do God's work with our money, he will give us more—more than we know what to do with. However, if we are constantly thinking, "What's in this for me?" or, "How little can I give and still get some credit for it?" we've derailed the blessing in our lives. God loves a cheerful giver. And he blesses a cheerful giver. To claim the blessing of wealth, you must abandon the notion to hoard it. Freely give, and you will freely receive.

4. THE BLESSING OF SECURITY

The fourth blessing pronounced on Asher is the blessing of *security*. Moses declared, "Thy shoes shall be iron and brass" (Deuteronomy 33:25). The reference to shoes of brass denotes peace or dominion. The person shod with brass is wearing steel-toed boots; nothing can harm him. That person will be secure, having nothing to fear.

Once again, this blessing is guaranteed also by Jesus for his servants. When sending out the seventy disciples on the first-ever, short-term mission trip, he told them, "Behold, I give unto you power to tread on serpents and scorpions, and over all the power of the enemy: and nothing shall by any means hurt you" (Luke 10:19). Paul echoed this thought in what should be the favorite verse of all who suffer adversity: "If God be for us, who can be against us?" (Romans 8:31). Nothing can separate us from the love and blessing of our God.

Well, that's not quite accurate. There is one thing that can hinder us from receiving the blessing of security, and that's a lack of faith, born of fear. You cannot be a fearful Christian and expect to move into new places with God. You cannot huddle in the back room and hope to miss the storm. When you are willing to go when God says, "Go," you have nothing to fear. What fear is keeping you held in place? When you think of taking on the challenge of doing God's will—serving, giving, working, claiming God's blessing—what holds you back? Fearful people are the least secure folk in the world. To realize the blessing of security, you must trust God. Do away with the mindset of self-protection. When God says, "Go," go boldly.

5. THE BLESSING OF STRENGTH

The fifth blessing pronounced on Asher is the blessing of *strength*. Moses declared, "And as thy days, so shall thy strength be" (Deuteronomy 33:25). What a beautiful promise! The natural way of things is that we grow weaker with each passing day. We have come to expect that as we age, we'll lose a little bit of ability. We'll lose a bit of mental sharpness. We'll give up some ground in our work or in our ministry. We won't be quite as effective as we once were. But the blessing of Asher establishes a spiritual law that countermands the natural one. As your days increase, your strength will also.

Impossible? Not for Moses, who didn't begin his real work of liberating the Israelites until he was eighty years of age. Not for Sarah who bore a child in her old age. Not for Caleb, one of the faith-filled spies who believed it was possible to conquer the land. Years later, at the end of the long and brutal conquest of

Canaan, Caleb was eighty-five years of age. Yet he went to Joshua with a bold request: "I am still as strong today as the day Moses sent me out; I'm just as vigorous to go out to battle now as I was then. Now give me this hill country that the LORD promised me that day. . . . the LORD helping me, I will drive them out just as he said" (Joshua 14:11–12 NIV). And that's exactly what he did.

It is true that we continue to struggle against our last enemy, which is death. But by God's grace, we can enjoy the blessing of strength far longer than we do. One reason we fail to enjoy this blessing is that we have accepted the idea that we must become weak and useless. We treat our bodies as if they were disposable rather than eternal. We love nothing better than having nothing to do, surrendering our God-given purpose for excessive leisure and time-wasting activities. We don't honor the temple of the Holy Spirit, which is our mortal body. To claim the blessing of strength, you must have a mindset of purpose and possibility. Do not surrender an inch of ground to the devil, who wants to render you useless. Work while the Lord gives you strength.

PRAYERS AS BIG AS GOD

What will it take for you to rise up and claim the blessing of Asher? What is the rut you must break out of? What mistake must you stop repeating? And what mistaken idea or wrong thinking is keeping you stuck in that place? Too many Christians miss out on the blessing of God because of their unholy attitude. Ingratitude, stinginess, complaining, lack of joy, pessimism, jealousy: these things are more than personality traits or foibles. They form a powerful block against the blessings of God. Moses knew that the people could not enter the Land of Promise until they got their minds right. They had to learn from the past, claim a new identity, and adopt a new mindset if they were to step into a new reality. The same is true for you.

Let your prayers be as big as God. Let your hopes be as vast as the heavens. Let your vision be as wide as eternity. Just as Abraham was blessed so that he could likewise bless the world, you too are blessed to be a blessing. When you think of yourself as a channel through which blessings pass rather than a bucket to hold little drops of God's grace, you will be blessed beyond measure. These things are promised to you; abundance, favor, wealth, security, and strength. Do you have the faith to accept them?

◇

THE SUCCESSFUL SEVEN

- Name an error you have fallen into more than once. Now state the lesson you have learned from it.

- Write down three things you understand about what it means to be blessed.

- Which of the blessings of Asher (abundance, favor, wealth, security, strength) do you need most? Name the hindrance you face in claiming it.

- Figure out how much money you have given to others in the past year, then make a plan to double that amount.

- Identify a person of whom you have been jealous and find a way to affirm that person.

- Pray, "Lord, expand my vision," then listen for his response.

- Memorize Galatians 3:29.

◇

7
The Power of Proximity

Therefore encourage one another and
build each other up, just as in fact you are doing.
—1 Thessalonians 5:11 NIV

THE WINNING CONCEPT

I must put myself in a position to win.

RIGHT PLACE, RIGHT TIME

Sometimes you benefit from being in the right place at the right time. That was the case for a couple from Burbank, California, who were moving out of their apartment. While carrying a box spring to the moving truck, they noticed a child tossing toys out of a third-story window in their building. The child's play turned deadly when the tot tried to climb out the window after his toys. Jennifer and Konrad Lightner sprang into action, hurling the box spring under the window just as the toddler fell. For a split second, the child's fall was arrested as he got tangled in a phone wire. That gave Konrad the opportunity to dash under the window just as the boy dropped into his waiting arms, landing them both on the box spring. Happily, the uninjured tyke was then reunited with his parents, who had been in another part of their apartment and unaware of what had happened.[24] That story is a great reminder of two important truths. First, it's vital to secure all windows when you have a small child at home. Second, good things happen when you are in the right place at the right time.

That truth is borne out by David, the young lad who happened to take supplies to his brothers serving in the army at the time when the giant Goliath was taunting the Israelites. Just being there gave him an opportunity to win the battle. It was the case also for Ruth, the young widow whose mother-in-law wisely suggested that she glean wheat in the field of Boaz, a godly man who first took notice of her, then took her under his protection, and ultimately married her. It seemed to be the life philosophy of Mary, sister of Lazarus, who made a habit of spending time with Jesus whenever he came to visit, rather than busying herself with household chores as her sister Martha did. Each of these biblical heroes understood the power of proximity. You can't win the battle unless you're at the battlefront. You won't learn the wisdom of the Master by washing pots in the kitchen. There is power in proximity.

As you move into the life of an overcomer, you must apply that principle. The ideas, people, and situations that you get next to will position you for success—or failure—in receiving God's

---

24. Ross A. Benson, "Quick Thinking Saves the Life of Three-Year-Old after Fall from Third Story Window," MyBurbank. com, March 17, 2014, http://myburbank.com/03/sections/policefire/fire/quick-thinking-saves-the-life-of-three-year-old-after-fall-from-second-story-window/.

blessings. You must put yourself in a position to win. Let's see how that principle played out in the life of a great biblical hero named Nehemiah, and we'll see how it can reinforce your own choice to win.

NEXT IN, NEHEMIAH

Nehemiah was in the right place at the right time, and he took advantage of the opportunity. The time was about 450 years before the birth of Christ. Many of God's people had returned to Jerusalem from their exile in Babylon. Nehemiah and some others remained in Persia, where Nehemiah had risen to the position of cupbearer to the king. When Nehemiah learned that the Jews living in Jerusalem were in distress, particularly because the walls of the city had been broken down, he was greatly troubled. Later, when Nehemiah went to serve the king, he noticed Nehemiah's low spirits and asked what was the matter. That put Nehemiah in a perfect position to make "the big ask." When the king heard that Jerusalem lay in ruins, he said to Jeremiah, "What is it you want?" (Nehemiah 2:4 NIV). Nehemiah wasted no time. He asked the king for a royal commission to go to Jerusalem and rebuild the city and the king said yes! Nehemiah went without delay and rebuilt the walls of Jerusalem. That's the power of proximity in action.

It's important to note that Nehemiah was not the first to attempt rebuilding the city. The first was Zerubbabel, who led the first group of exiles to return from Babylon and began rebuilding the temple. However, Zerubbabel was not able to completely restore Jerusalem. The walls of the city lay in ruins for another ninety years. Then along came Nehemiah, who was placed in a high position as cupbearer to the king. Because he was in the right place at the right time, he got a great opportunity. And Nehemiah made the most of that opportunity, completing the restoration of the city's walls in just fifty-two days. That would be an astounding feat even today, with the aid of power equipment. Yet Nehemiah was able to mobilize a workforce in the face of great opposition from Jerusalem's hostile neighbors and finish the job in record time, entirely with manual labor. How did he do it? By leveraging the power of proximity.

THE POWER OF NEXT

Nehemiah understood that there is power not only in being next to a powerful person like the king of Persia, but also in being next to diligent coworkers. He understood that people work better and more efficiently when side-by-side with likeminded teammates. Nehemiah leveraged that power in organizing the workers on the wall. Here's how it's stated in Nehemiah 3:1–4:

> *Then Eliashib the high priest rose up with his brethren the priests, and they builded the sheep gate; they sanctified it, and set up the doors of it; even unto the tower of Meah they sanctified it, unto the tower of Hananeel. And next unto him builded the men of Jericho. And next to them builded Zaccur the son of Imri. But the fish gate did the sons of Hassenaah build, who also laid the beams thereof, and set up the doors thereof, the locks thereof, and the bars thereof. And next unto them repaired Meremoth the son of Urijah, the son of Koz. And next unto them repaired Meshullam the son of Berechiah, the son of Meshezabeel. And next unto them repaired Zadok the son of Baana.*

Notice how many times the word *next* appears in these few verses. *Next* means adjacent, connected to, or close by. The Hebrew word for next indicates a position above or over someone but with a hand extended downward. It gives the picture of being within arm's reach. So each man worked independently but was close enough to the others to reach out if there was a need. By being in close proximity, they were able to protect one another, encourage one another, and lend each other a hand. This was more than simple teamwork or camaraderie. Nehemiah's selection of people and his placement of them in their tasks shows that he carefully linked one person's work with his neighbors to create a strength and efficiency that was greater than the sum of its parts. We derive great power by being next to the right people.

That's true in everyday life as well as in a major project such as rebuilding the temple. When you're among good friends, you feed off their affirmation and encouragement. When you're in the company of talented people, it inspires you to do your best. Spending time with people of faith strengthens your ability to trust God. Happy, optimistic, hopeful people lift your spirits, sometimes indirectly. Just being around them makes you feel better. As a result, you have more energy, are more tolerant, and are better able to face your challenges.

This proximity principle has a negative side though. There is power in being connected with positive people, but there's weakness in being close to those who are negative. If you place yourself near the wrong people, you can go down with them. If there is no one willing and able to reach out to you when you're down, you won't recover from failure or adversity. If you link up with friends who have a me-first attitude, you've tied a boat anchor to your dreams.

You need to be around people who will do for you what Jesus did for Simon Peter when he got nervous while walking on water. When Peter began to sink beneath the waves, Jesus "stretched forth his hand" and pulled Simon out of the turbulent waters (Matthew 14:31). That's the power of proximity. You gain power and possibility by being next to Jesus, obviously, but also by being next to his people.

God is looking for people who will stretch out a hand to one another, back one another up, encourage each other, and hold each other accountable. By seeking out hopeful, faithful people, you lift your own vision and gain perseverance. Who are you next to? Take a close look at the people, places, and situations that get the most of your time. You are certain to become more like them over time.

THE POWER OF AFTER

Nehemiah used the word *next* sixteen times, and that use was intentional. He also used the word *after* sixteen times. Why? Because while you are beside some people, you are also behind and in front of others. You came after someone, and someone else will come after you. Pay close attention to who is in front of you and to who is behind. You're being led by one, and you're guiding the other.

Elisha and Elijah illustrate the power of being next in line. When the great prophet Elijah had finished his ministry, God took him up to heaven in a whirlwind. Before that happened, Elijah urged his protégé, Elisha, to remain behind while Elijah traveled on. Knowing that Elijah's departure was near, Elisha refused to stay behind. He insisted on sticking close to his master. Later,

Elijah asked, "Tell me, what can I do for you before I am taken from you?" (2 Kings 2:9 NIV). Because of his stubborn refusal to leave Elijah's side, Elisha found himself in a position to make a big ask of his own. He said, "Let me inherit a double portion of your spirit" (verse 9). That decision was not Elijah's to make. But God did indeed grant the request, and Elisha became the successor of the great Elijah. Elisha came next, in part, because of the power of proximity.

You have mentors whether you chose them intentionally or not. There are people in your church, workplace, or school whom you admire and respect. If they are worth following, you'll gain strength by that association. But if you hitch your wagon to the wrong horse, you'll be dragged off in the wrong direction. You don't want to inherit a double portion of anything from a person of low character or weak faith. Learn from those who will build something positive into your life. Read the books of great leaders, thinkers, and prayers. Choose a church where the pastor preaches solid biblical truth and lives it out in everyday life. Find a mentor who has overcome the same adversity you're facing and learn everything you can from that person. If they were the first to overcome, you can be next.

There is great power in being near a powerful person, as Nehemiah was. There is power also in being next to or in following after those who can help you succeed. Nehemiah understood that when he doled out assignments for rebuilding the wall. Let's take a closer look at the people Nehemiah placed next to one another. Their seamless cooperation and mutual support was a key to success in rebuilding the wall in just fifty-two days. We can learn something from them.

THREE PEOPLE TO GET NEXT TO

There is a difference between building and rebuilding. To build something is to establish it, to start from scratch and create something solid and useful. That's important. We like to think that we're building for the future and creating something enduring for our families. We need to be diligent in that. We want our lives to be a solid foundation for the next generation. We are all builders in that sense.

But sometimes we must repair rather than rebuild. To repair is to put right, to restore to good order. It's interesting to note that the word *build* appears only four times in Nehemiah 3, but the word *repair* is used thirty-five times. Nehemiah was engaged in rebuilding. The walls had been built centuries before, but they had been torn down. Nehemiah's task was to rebuild them. He wasn't trying to invent something, but to restore what had been destroyed.

Like Nehemiah, we're engaged in rebuilding. God established a perfect pattern for life, but that pattern was disrupted when Adam and Eve ate the forbidden fruit, allowing sin to enter the world. We live now in a world broken by disease, violence, tragedy, and death. The adversity you now face is a direct result of that. It stems either from sin in your life, from the sinful actions of others, or from the broken condition of the world. That's why Jesus came to give us life, to rebuild what the devil has destroyed. We are involved in the work of restoration. We want to repair the damage done in families by unfaithfulness or violence. We want to rebuild financial strength and good credit. We want to see marriages restored, communities revitalized, and health and strength returned to those who suffer. If we're to be involved in this great work of rebuilding, we can take a lesson from the crew that Nehemiah appointed to repair the great walls surrounding Jerusalem. Here are three people to stay close to as you rebuild your life.

ELIASHIB: CONFIDENCE

The first rebuilder we meet is Eliashib. He was the high priest and he and his company of priests rebuilt a portion of the wall that included the sheep gate. What's interesting is the meaning of this builder's name. Eliashib means God will restore. The emphasis is entirely positive—God *will* restore. It isn't that he may do so or that he can do so. He will restore. And through Eliashib, God did exactly that.

When you're trying to move beyond adversity, it is vital to maintain an attitude of hope and confidence. Through the prophet Joel, the Lord promised to restore the years that the locusts have eaten (Joel 2:25). That's a beautiful promise of restoration. And Jesus said, "Behold, I make all things new" (Revelation 21:5). What have you lost? What has been aborted, stunted, or removed from your life? God promises to restore that, and he will do it. Obviously, this does not mean that you'll return to being a child so you can relive the "lost" years of your life. Some consequences of sin are permanent in this life and some missed opportunities won't come again. However, God can and will restore relationships and health and finances and peace. The joy that has been lost in your life will return.

As you set out to rebuild your life, choose a workstation near Eliashib. Get a dose of his confidence. Seek out the people who have a positive outlook, who move through life with hope rather than a spirit of resignation. Everyone doubts from time to time, but don't put yourself in close proximity to the perpetually doubtful. Pessimists won't help you win. Stick close to people of faith and vision. There will be times when you need to reach out to them, and they can extend an open hand of confidence. Stay in close proximity to hope. That will help you overcome doubt and discouragement in your life. It will enable you to keep building.

ZACCUR: MOTIVATION

Next to Eliashib and his crew were the men of Jericho, and next to them was Zaccur. The name *Zaccur* means to mention often, to remember, or to reflect. I like to think that Zaccur lived up to his name and reflected often on the past. If so, that reflection would have provided a strong motivation for Zaccur and his companions to keep working. When we remember what God has done in the past, it motivates us for the future.

During Zaccur's lifetime, there may have been no great exploits to remember. It had been 90 years since Zerubbabel tried to rebuild Jerusalem, and nearly 150 years since the city had been destroyed. God had allowed the exiles to return to Jerusalem, but not much had happened since then. However, Zaccur would have known all about the great things God had done in the past thanks to Ezra. Ezra was a teacher of the law who had led a second group of exiles back to Jerusalem just prior to the time of Nehemiah. Ezra also brought back the teaching of the Torah, the first five books of the Old Testament, to the Jewish people. Because of Ezra's teaching, Zaccur could have recalled the time of Abraham and the great promise of God's blessing. He would have heard often of the Passover, when God delivered his people from slavery in Egypt. Zaccur could have reflected on the law of God and the words of the prophets. He could have imagined the parting of the Red Sea and crossing the Jordan River. Thinking about the glorious work of God in the past would have motivated Zaccur to keep rebuilding.

When you're faced with a huge task, the work can seem daunting, even impossible. If you are stuck in some negative circumstance, it may be disheartening to see all the things that have to change. When you're looking at a huge pile of stones, it's hard to muster the energy to build them into a wall. That's when it helps to remember what God has already done for you. Recall the fact that God has given you life—and one more day to live and breathe. Where there is life, there is hope. Remember that God has forgiven your sins. Reflect often on the grace he has already shown to you. Don't lose sight of any miracles God has already performed. Remember such experiences often, like miracles of healing or the provision of food or material things. Look to your past; it will motivate your future.

When you are engaged in the formidable task of rebuilding your life, position yourself next to Zaccur. Listen to him recount the goodness of God and reflect with him on all the good things God has already done in your life. That memory will reinvigorate you and motivate you for the future.

HASSENAAH: FOCUS

Next to Zaccur were the sons of Hassenaah, which means direct or to the point. If these sons lived up to their name, they were a no-nonsense crew who didn't waste time on small talk. They were focused, deliberate, and undistracted. I imagine these men taking short breaks and never dallying around the water cooler. They were all business, highly attentive to the task at hand.

It's common to begin a major project with lots of enthusiasm only to see that enthusiasm wane when the going gets tough.

You may have experienced this, even when working on small or insignificant projects. When you have a job to finish, you start out by diving right in. By break time, you're getting a little tired. You may take a long lunch in an effort to get your focus back. By midafternoon you're checking email every five minutes, hoping someone will distract you from your work. Focus evaporates quickly.

That can be doubly true when the project is rebuilding your life. The problems you face are deeply rooted and cannot be overcome quickly. It may take years to lose the weight that you have accumulated over time. A mountain of debt can be chipped away, but not with a single paycheck. Restoring a marriage can take months of patient, loving communication. Don't become distracted. If you do, you'll find yourself falling back to the beginning. If you repeat that cycle of enthusiasm and boredom enough times, you may give up altogether.

Find the sons of Hassenaah and work alongside them. If you're serious about restoring your health, stick close to people who have mastered the art of eating right and getting proper exercise. They won't be distracted by a Big Mac, and you won't either. If you need financial focus, spend your time around those who conserve their money. They won't get bored and start buying lottery tickets, and they won't binge shop using a credit card. That discipline will rub off if you will make them your companions. Find the people who are focused on the same goals you are and rebuild your life alongside them. Leverage the power of proximity to sharpen your focus.

YOU'RE NEXT

Several other workers are named in Nehemiah 3. Next to Hassenaah was Meremoth, whose name means the flame of God.

Next to him was Meshullam, whose name means the blessing of God. Next to him was Zadok, meaning just. Rebuilding the wall was not accomplished by a single leader, Nehemiah, nor by a single builder like Eliashib or Hassenaah. It took all of them, working side by side, each offering a particular strength and each lending a hand to the others when needed. It was one person next to another, next to another, next to another. And here's the really important thing: you're next in line. You stand behind Nehemiah but ahead of the next generation. You are shoulder-to-shoulder with your family, friends, and companions. It's your turn now.

The apostle Paul writes about this experience in Ephesians 4:16, where he says, "From whom the whole body fitly joined together and compacted by that which every joint supplieth, according to the effectual working in the measure of every part, maketh increase of the body unto the edifying of itself in love." That's a description of us in the church. The power of proximity is magnified as we, fitted together like the parts of a body, leverage the strengths of one another. This metaphor was Paul's way of reminding us that we are stronger together, that we need one another, that we don't dare attempt this life alone. When we stick close to one another, we put ourselves in a position to grow—and we help others do the same.

What about you? Are you leveraging the power of proximity by sticking close to hopeful, faithful people who can lend a hand and bolster your strength? Or are you multiplying your distractions and weakening your resolve by standing alongside negative people or in questionable situations? Nehemiah understood that great opportunities come your way when you're in the right place at the right time. Choose your companions wisely. Latch onto wise and successful mentors. Leverage the power of proximity and put yourself in a position to win.

◇

THE SUCCESSFUL SEVEN

- Name the five people you spend the most time with, then state whether each of them is *empowering* you or *distracting* you.

- Take a self-inventory to answer this question: Do I need more help with confidence, motivation, or focus? Name one person who could assist you in each area.

- State the primary difficulty you are trying to overcome, then name one person you know who has successfully faced that challenge. Set an appointment to speak with them.

- List the places where you spend the most time during the week, then list the things you encounter there that (a) help you overcome adversity and (b) create tension, stress, or temptation. Name one way you can minimize the negative effect and maximize the positive effect of each environment.

- Identify a person to whom you might be a mentor, then offer to spend some time with that person.

- List your current involvements in church (anything from no involvement, to attending, to volunteering). Name one way you can deepen your involvement for the purpose of strengthening your focus on overcoming.

- Memorize 1 Thessalonians 5:11.

◇

8

Even When You Are Weak You Are Strong

*Therefore I take pleasure in infirmities, in reproaches,
in necessities, in persecutions, in distresses for Christ's sake:
for when I am weak, then am I strong.*
—2 Corinthians 12:10

THE WINNING CONCEPT

God works through my weaknesses, not my strengths.

UNLIKELY HEROES

Sometimes there's just nothing you can do, right? There are some situations in which you are so overwhelmed or help-less that you must accept things as they are. There is hunger in the world. Bad things happen. No one person is powerful enough to bring a change. Sometimes you are better off to admit that you're beaten, right?

Don't tell that to eight-year-old Cayden Taipalus, a third-grader from Howell, Michigan, who saw that another child at his school was going hungry and decided to do something about it. When Cayden observed a boy in the lunch line putting down his tray because he couldn't pay for the food, he went into action. What could an eight-year-old do? He collected cans and bottles for recycling to raise money to pay for school lunches. His first week's effort yielded $64, enough to pay for nearly 150 lunches. Friends and neighbors heard about the campaign and decided to help. Thanks to local radio and social media, the effort got wide attention and drew donations from as far away as Hong Kong. A week later, the campaign had produced over $10,800. "We went from just paying off his elementary school to paying off the entire Livingston County," Cayden's mom said. And the initiative spread to other school districts, inspiring hundreds to help with lunch costs for kids who can't afford them.[25] Maybe the powerless do have some power after all.

A nine-year-old named Ken thinks so. This little boy living in the Philippines had a heart for stray animals and wanted to begin a shelter, but his father discouraged him from thinking big. The boy's dad said that it would take a lot of money and twenty years to start a shelter. That was something "only grown-ups" could do. Ken disagreed and started feeding stray dogs outside his garage. He also made a fundraising poster and posted some photos of the dogs online. Before long he had raised some $1,500, enough to lease a 10,000-square-foot lot for one year. After a lot of work and many more donations, the Happy Animals Club has two large pens, two apartments, and an annex. It is a registered nonprofit

25. Kami Dimitrova, "Eight-Year-Old's 'Heart of Gold' Helps Pay Off Student's Lunch Debt," ABC News, March 3, 2014, http://abcnews.go.com/US/year-olds-heart-gold-helps-pay-off-students/story?id=22756619, and Danika Fears, "'Good-hearted boy': 8-year-old pays off overdue lunch accounts," Today.com, March 4, 2014, http://www.today.com/news/good-hearted-boy-8-year-old-pays-overdue-lunch-accounts-2D79314690.

organization in the Philippines, managed by Ken and a staff of volunteers. They take in dogs that would otherwise be euthanized by local authorities.[26]

These feel-good stories illustrate an important principle for anyone who faces the challenge of bettering their life. Moving beyond years of failure and inertia may have left you feeling weak, helpless, and stuck. If so, learn this principle: God favors the weak. The very moment when you feel the smallest and most helpless is the moment you are most likely to receive a huge dose of God's blessing. "But God hath chosen the foolish things of the world to confound the wise; and God hath chosen the weak things of the world to confound the things which are mighty" (1 Corinthians 1:27). In this chapter we'll see how this principle is rooted in Scripture, beginning with the blessing given to Benjamin, the youngest son of Jacob. We'll also see how the Benjamin Blessing applies to your life right now.

THE GREAT ROLE REVERSAL

In our way of thinking, being first is everything. There may be no more despised label than that of *loser*. We are taught from an early age to compete for top honors. Everybody wants to win. One of the obstacles we face in overcoming the problems in our lives is the feeling, and sometimes the reality, that we are stuck in last place. Our problems have put us behind others intellectually, financially, or professionally. We've failed in some way, and that failure has become a ball and chain that keeps us from moving forward. When you're on top, you have lots of opportunity. When you're last in line, you must simply accept your lot.

---

26. "Origins: The Happy Animals Club Story," Happy Animals Club website, n.d., https://www.happyanimalsclub.org/origins.

That may be true from a human perspective, but there is a spiritual reality that turns this way of thinking on its head. For Jesus said, "The last shall be first, and the first last" (Matthew 20:16). Throughout Scripture we see that God often promotes the smallest over the largest and places the last in front of the first. One of the first times we see this is in the blessing given to Benjamin by his brother Joseph. It took place after Joseph's brothers came to him in Egypt, looking for food because of a famine in the land of Canaan. Twice during the episode, Joseph showed special favor to his brother Benjamin, the youngest of the brood. The first occasion was when the brothers sat down to eat together. At that point, the sons of Jacob had not recognized that Joseph was their long-lost brother. "And [Joseph] took and sent messes unto them from before him: but Benjamin's mess was five times so much as any of theirs. And they drank, and were merry with him" (Genesis 43:34). The second time was after Joseph had made himself known to his brothers. He gave them gifts to send them on their way back to Canaan. "To all of them he gave each man changes of raiment; but to Benjamin he gave three hundred pieces of silver, and five changes of raiment" (Genesis 45:22). Joseph showed greater favor to his youngest brother than to the oldest, which was unusual in that culture. Why would he have done that?

You might think it was because Benjamin, being the youngest, had had no part in the brothers' plot to sell Joseph into slavery many years earlier. Or you might think that it was because Joseph and Benjamin were full brothers, having the same mother, Rachel. It's more likely that Joseph understood that Benjamin occupied a special place in the family because he had been blessed by their father, Jacob. Of all Jacob's sons, Benjamin was the only one to be born in Canaan, the land promised to Abraham's descendants. Also, Benjamin's mother died just after giving birth to him. With her last breath, she named him Benoni, which means son of my trouble. But Jacob immediately changed the boy's name to Benjamin, which means son of my right hand. By changing his name to Benjamin, Jacob elevated his youngest son to a position of power, his "right hand man." The last child had been placed ahead of the first. The youngest had become the greatest. That is the Benjamin Blessing in a nutshell: The last become first, and the weak become strong.

THE POWER OF A NEW NAME

This repositioning of Benjamin from last to first has great implications for you. To begin, let's examine the aspect of renaming. Renaming is a powerful symbolic statement in any era, but especially in biblical times. Remember that Abram's name was changed to Abraham, signifying that he would become the father of many nations (Genesis 17:5). Also, Saul's name was changed to Paul—a Jewish name exchanged for a Gentile one—to show that he had a new mission to reach the Gentiles for Christ (Acts 13:9). Today, a change of name signifies a change of identity, which is why people commonly change their names when getting married or converting to a new faith. Renaming Benoni as Benjamin wasn't a simple preference for a name that sounded better. It showed that Benjamin had been elevated above his brothers. The name given by Rachel, his mother, did not stand. Benjamin's true identity was determined by Jacob, his father.

Too often, we allow our "Mother," meaning the church, to pronounce our identity, and it often comes out something like "child of my trouble." Sadly, we in the church may uncharitably judge our brothers and sisters because of their past deeds or their present circumstances. We may pronounce a name over them that emphasizes their failure rather than their future. Though we may never say them out loud, labels like *sinner, addict, tramp,* or *abuser* may run though our minds—and may stick in another person's heart. One reason we remain stuck is that we too easily accept those labels from others, even from people in the church. When you honestly believe that your identity is "troubled person" or "wayward child" or "hot mess," you're certain to act as helpless as you feel.

Jacob gave his son a better name, and your Father has given you a better name also. Throughout this book we've seen the powerful impact of your sense of identity on your ability to overcome. It bears repeating that you must gain your identity from what God says about you, not from what others say—even others within the church. God alone determines who you are. And he calls you beloved (Romans 8:39), chosen (Ephesians 1:4), forgiven (Ephesians 1:6–8), accepted (Romans 15:7), child of God (John 1:12), God's masterpiece (Ephesians 2:10). Latch onto your new identity in Christ. You are not helpless just because other people say you are. You have been empowered by God to overcome.

THE POWER OF A HIGHER LAW

Benjamin may have had a new identity thanks to his new name, but by the customs of his time he was still the least member of the family. The blessing always passed to the oldest son. That was the law of the times. However, a new law was put into effect, a higher law that superseded human convention.

The law of gravity is an immutable law of science. It works every time, and nothing can overturn that law. When you drop a bowling ball, it's going to fall down. You may declare that it won't, but wishing won't make it so. When you let go of a heavy object, you'd best move your feet. However, the law of aerodynamics is an immutable law also, and it supersedes the law of gravity. When air moves over an airfoil, it produces lift every time. So an airplane can move up, even though the law of gravity remains in effect. The second law takes precedence over the first, even though the first law remains in effect.

The same is true in spiritual things. The law demands that the wages of sin is death (Romans 6:23). That's true every time. However, there is a higher law at work. The law of the Spirit who gives life has set you free from the law of sin and death (Romans 8:2). The law of the spirit takes precedence over the law of death. In Christ, the guilty become not guilty. The weak become strong. The last become first. When you came to Christ, the law of the Spirit took precedence over everything in your life. Your past was nullified. You were given a new identity and a new future!

That's important to remember when you feel powerless to change your life. Looking at things objectively—that is, looking only at the physical reality of your situation—you may be help-less to change your circumstances, stuck in last place. You may be the oldest person working in an industry dominated by young people. You may be the poorest person in your neighborhood. You may be at the bottom level of graduates from your school—or perhaps you didn't graduate. In every area you can think of, you don't stand a chance.

But there is a higher law at work. According to God's *modus operandi*—his method of operating—you are not stuck where you are. You are elevated to the highest. You are forgiven, loved, and free. You are empowered. You are able to overcome. You have been given a new identity, declared to be God's right-hand person.

When it comes to reconciling your marriage or getting out of debt or overcoming a dreaded illness, you may feel as helpless as an eight-year-old boy standing in the lunch line with no money. But remember the blessing of Benjamin! God empowers those who appear to be weak. He sets aside the troubles that surround them and creates a new reality. Do not accept the idea that you are helpless, and do not allow shame over past failures to paralyze you. Stop seeing yourself as the smallest, weakest, or least likely to succeed. Remember that the law of the Spirit reverses the law of sin and death. You're no longer living under the old rules. You may be small in your own eyes, but you are serving a big God and you are blessed. You are free to rise. Free to become the person God intends you to be.

FAVOR IN WEAKNESS

Most people find shame in their weaknesses. You may have noticed that people who have difficulty walking often try to hide it. They may use a cane or walker when nobody's looking, but they try to do without them when others are nearby. Those who have difficulty hearing often deny the problem, refusing to be fitted with a hearing aid until friends and loved ones insist upon it. When we make a mistake, our first impulse is to deny it or to make an excuse for it. We don't like to appear weak, incompetent, foolish, or helpless. That's odd because we all have shortcomings. We all stumble sometimes, so there should be no shame in admitting it. So why do we hide our weaknesses?

The reason is that we have a deeply rooted sense of shame due to the original sin that affects every one of us. Remember that when Adam and Eve committed that first sin in the garden of Eden, their response was to hide in shame (Genesis 3:10). We all feel a bit of that shame, and it is exposed whenever we are forced to acknowledge our human frailty. As a result, we overcompensate. We pretend that we're always self-sufficient and never wrong. We have convinced ourselves that only the strong will survive, only the most competitive companies will succeed, only the top-performing employees are valued. We have come to accept the idea of the survival of the fittest, and we fear anything that makes us feel weak or helpless.

Scripture gives us a different view of strength and weakness. The very things that we eagerly try to hide, God wants to use for his glory. For God delights in using the weaker things in this world to bring glory to himself. As the apostle Paul said, "But God hath chosen the foolish things of the world to confound the wise; and God hath chosen the weak things of the world to confound the things which are mighty" (1 Corinthians 1:27). Little Benjamin, the weakest of the brothers and the smallest of the twelve tribes of Israel demonstrates that point.

PROTECTION FOR THE WEAK

Before the twelve tribes entered the Promised Land, Moses pronounced this blessing on the descendants of Benjamin: "The beloved of the Lord shall dwell in safety by him; and the Lord shall cover him all the day long, and he shall dwell between his shoulders" (Deuteronomy 33:12). Size and strength were equated in the thinking of that culture, so it's significant that God loves even the weakest and promises him protection. Benjamin, though virtually at the mercy of others, would dwell in safety. The image of dwelling between the Lord's shoulders is powerful. Picture giving a little child a ride on your shoulders, one leg draped over each one. That's the protection God promises to the weakest, and that's the protection he promises to you in your weakness.

Throughout Scripture God promises protection for the helpless. There are so many verses that demonstrate this that it's impossible to list them all here, but this sampling reveals the overwhelming concern God has for the weak.

- "Defend the poor and fatherless: do justice to the afflicted and needy. Deliver the poor and needy: rid them out of the hand of the wicked" (Psalm 82:3–4).

- "Learn to do well; seek judgment, relieve the oppressed, judge the fatherless, plead for the widow" (Isaiah 1:17).

- "If thou forbear to deliver them that are drawn unto death, and those that are ready to be slain; If thou sayest, Behold, we knew it not; doth not he that pondereth the heart consider it? and he that keepeth thy soul, doth not he know it? and shall not he render to every man according to his works?" (Proverbs 24:11–12).

- "He shall spare the poor and needy, and shall save the souls of the needy" (Psalm 72:13).

- "And oppress not the widow, nor the fatherless, the stranger, nor the poor; and let none of you imagine evil against his brother in your heart" (Zechariah 7:10).

- "Take heed that ye despise not one of these little ones; for I say unto you, That in heaven their angels do always behold the face of my Father which is in heaven" (Matthew 18:10).

- "He that oppresseth the poor reproacheth his Maker: but he that honoureth him hath mercy on the poor" (Proverbs 14:31).

- "Then shall they also answer him, saying, Lord, when saw we thee an hungred, or athirst, or a stranger, or naked, or sick, or in prison, and did not minister unto thee? Then shall he answer them, saying, Verily I say unto you, Inasmuch as ye did it not to one of the least of these, ye did it not to me" (Matthew 25:44–45).

God has a soft spot for little children, widows, refugees, the homeless, the poor—in short, anyone who is helpless or at the mercy of others. Those who lack money, power, and social status may rate at the bottom of the world's concerns, but they top God's list. So when you feel at your most vulnerable, you are in for a special blessing from God. When you need help the most, he promises to be right there to provide it. That's the Blessing of Benjamin, and it's your blessing too.

EMPOWERMENT FOR THE WEAK

The apostle Paul suffered a particular form of weakness. Nobody knows exactly what it was, but Paul referred to it as his "thorn in the flesh" (2 Corinthians 12:7). Some people think it was a speech impediment like stuttering, or a chronic illness such as epilepsy. You can imagine how frustrating something like that would have been for a leader. On occasions when he needed to be at his best, such as preaching in the synagogue or defending himself against the civil authorities, Paul was vulnerable to this infirmity that may have left him speechless or powerless. This was a great burden to Paul. Three times he begged God to remove it from him. You can imagine the anguish he felt when the answer was no each time.

Yet because of this limitation, Paul discovered an important aspect of the Benjamin Blessing: there is strength in weakness. Paul realized that because of his personal limitations, he could never claim to be invincible or pretend that his success came from his own ability. The fact that he had such a prominent handicap proved that any success he had must come from God. He put it like this: "But [God] said to me, 'My grace is sufficient for you, for my power is made perfect in weakness.' Therefore I will boast all the more gladly about my weaknesses, so that Christ's power may rest on me. That is why, for Christ's sake, I delight in weaknesses, in insults, in hardships, in persecutions, in difficulties. For when I am weak, then I am strong" (2 Corinthians 12:9–10 NIV).

Do you see the Benjamin Blessing at work here? Not only does God promise to protect the weak but he also uses their weakness as a form of strength. When we quit trying to hide or deny our weaknesses, God is then able to work in us and through us. In the end, we find that the very things we thought would hold us back can become our greatest source of strength.

If you suffer from a physical ailment or a chronic condition, don't wait until you're healed to start overcoming the obstacles in your life. Learn to see your limitations as an opportunity for God to reveal his strength. People who can't walk can still travel. Those who cannot see can still write books. Your "weakness" can become a strength in that it forces you to rely on God rather than yourself. And it will give you deeper insight into the human condition and greater empathy for those who suffer. Those are true strengths. The prophet Joel said, "Beat your plowshares into swords and your pruninghooks into spears: let the weak say,

I am strong" (Joel 3:10). In other words, don't wait until you have all the "weapons" you need to overcome the adversity in your life. Use the tools that God has placed within your reach. You are stronger than you think.

HELPING THE WEAK

One of the best things you can do to move forward in life is to help someone else do the same thing. This is a well-known principle, and it applies in every area of life. If you are struggling to learn math, teach what you are learning to someone else. You will both master it. If you are trying to break an addiction, counsel someone else who is also trying to quit. In saving them from temptation, you will also save yourself. This too is part of the Benjamin Blessing, the inversion of weakness and strength. Paul wrote, "I have shewed you all things, how that so laboring ye ought to support the weak, and to remember the words of the Lord Jesus, how he said, It is more blessed to give than to receive" (Acts 20:35). There is a blessing in giving—of your time, talent, or treasure—to those in need. When you help the weak, you help yourself.

It's not that we do this for selfish reasons. Paul warns against that very thing: "We then that are strong ought to bear the infirmities of the weak, and not to please ourselves" (Romans 15:1). When you are ministering to the weak it should not be from a desire to make yourself look good. If that is your motivation, you will burn out very quickly. Instead, find the joy in helping others, and let that become a source of strength.

THE LITTLE CHAMPION

Benjamin was the youngest of the sons of Jacob, and his descendants formed the smallest of the twelve tribes of Israel. But though he was the baby brother, Benjamin was superior to his siblings in many ways, and history bears that out. The blessing pronounced on Benjamin when Jacob changed his name from "son of my trouble" to "son of my right hand" had a powerful effect. On his deathbed, Jacob gave a more specific blessing to Benjamin. He said, "Benjamin shall ravin as a wolf: in the morning he shall devour the prey, and at night he shall divide the spoil" (Deuteronomy 49:27). In that blessing, Jacob indicated that Benjamin would receive a great reward ("spoil"), but he would have to fight for it. Jacob said, in effect, "You will be fierce, but you will win—and you'll have something to show for it."

That's exactly what happened. During the conquest of Canaan, the sons of Benjamin were given fourteen cities with their villages (Joshua 18:28). And the psalmist wrote, "Bless ye God in the congregations, even the Lord, from the fountain of Israel. There is little Benjamin with their ruler, the princes of Judah and their council, the princes of Zebulun, and the princes of Naphtali. Thy God hath commanded thy strength: strengthen, O God, that which thou hast wrought for us" (Psalm 68:26–28). There is "little Benjamin," listed first, ahead of Judah again! Benjamin became one of the rulers of Israel.

That was literally true when Saul, a Benjamanite, became the first king over Israel. Saul turned out to be a man of low character who made a poor king. Even so, Benjamin had the first oppor-

tunity to rule. Also, Mordecai and Esther were from the tribe of
Benjamin. When Esther had an opportunity to save the Jewish
people from destruction at the risk of her own life, Mordecai told
her, "For if thou altogether holdest thy peace at this time, then
shall there enlargement and deliverance arise to the Jews from
another place; but thou and thy father's house shall be destroyed:
and who knoweth whether thou art come to the kingdom for
such a time as this?" (Esther 4:14). Mordecai understood that
God didn't need them—he could save the people in any number
of ways—but Esther, though an unlikely hero, was given a unique
opportunity. She had been raised from the status of lowly refugee to the exalted position of queen of Persia for "such a time as
this." Talk about a Benjamin Blessing! God granted a great victory
through the faithfulness of an immigrant girl who was moved to
the head of the line.

The apostle Paul was from the tribe of Benjamin too. He illustrates the Benjamin Blessing in reverse. Paul had been one of the
leading men of his time: "of the stock of Israel, of the tribe of Benjamin, an Hebrew of the Hebrews; as touching the law, a Pharisee;
Concerning zeal, persecuting the church; touching the righteous-
ness which is in the law, blameless" (Philippians 3:5–6). Paul was
in first place in every category that counted, a leader among leaders. Yet before God could use Paul, he had to be knocked from his
high horse—literally! On the Damascus Road, Christ appeared to
Paul, blinding him and knocking him to the ground. Only when
Paul discovered the power of weakness could he become a strong
leader in the church. He later wrote, "For when I am weak, then
I am strong."

The point of recounting these biblical examples is to prove a simple point: the Benjamin Blessing is powerful, effective, and real. God really does invert the natural order of things, putting the last people in first place and humbling those who are more prominent. God does favor the small, protect the weak, and perform some of his greatest acts through the least likely people. You may be afraid to trust this principle, but it is entirely reliable and borne out on every page of Scripture. If you are painfully aware of your own weakness, failures, and shortcomings, that's a good thing. It means that you are humble enough for God to elevate you. Don't allow your failures and shortcomings to keep you from stepping into God's glorious future. For when you are weak, then you are strong.

◇

THE SUCCESSFUL SEVEN

- List the things about you and your situation that seem hopeless, then write a biblical promise next to each one.

- Write a one or two sentence description of the Benjamin Blessing, then explain that blessing to someone you know.

- What are your three greatest weaknesses? How might God use them as strengths?

- What are your three greatest strengths? In what ways have you been tempted to rely on them rather than God?

- Identify a person who is suffering or in need and offer some form of tangible help.

- Ask a friend or mentor to hold you accountable to a "no whining" rule. Say, "Whenever you hear me saying 'I can't,' point it out to me."

- Memorize 2 Corinthians 12:10.

◇

PART 3
Profiles in Overcoming

This section will inspire you to move forward in faith based on the examples of great biblical heroes. You'll see that with God, nothing is impossible, and you'll be inspired to persevere in your journey. You will make these discoveries:

God has me here for a reason.

I gain by giving to others.

I grow stronger through hard times.

There are better days ahead.

When you lift your vision to see the possibilities God has for you, despite your current circumstances, you'll be empowered to move forward into a new life.

◇

◇

9

The Reason for Your Season

To every thing there is a season,
and a time to every purpose under the heaven.
—Ecclesiastes 3:1

THE WINNING ATTITUDE

God has me here for a reason.

THE MOST BRILLIANT YEAR

What's the worst thing you could imagine happening to you? For many people, that would be something like the nightmare suffered by Alex Lewis, a British man who came down with what he thought was a routine sore throat. In reality, the then thirty-four-year-old husband and father had contracted a Group A streptococcus infection, which produced blood poisoning and ate away at his flesh. Within a month he had lost both legs, his left arm, and the flesh around his lips, leaving a gaping hole where his mouth had been. After six months in the hospital, he had undergone more than one hundred hours of surgery, had over thirty skin grafts, lost his right hand, and had part of his shoulder grafted to his face to form a new mouth. He now weighs just eighty-four pounds, depends on a wheelchair to move around, and has had his facial appearance permanently altered by skin grafting.

Yet Alex, who now operates an interior design company said, "The year I lost my limbs was the most brilliant of my life. . . . The man I was isn't necessarily the man I am today—in a good way, I think."

Think for a moment. Do you think you could say something like that after a year of painful surgeries that left you, literally, half the person you had been? If you're thinking that reaction is unusual, you're probably not alone. "Brilliant" is not a term most of us would use to describe the most difficult season of our lives.

Yet Alex's optimistic statement does not mean that he takes delight in suffering. Instead, it is focused on the result that suffering produced in his life. Prior to the illness, he'd been unmotivated. He drank to excess and had been through a series of jobs that led nowhere. He had become a couch potato. After the illness, he quit drinking, began to eat a healthier diet, and returned to work doing interior design. He's also helping researchers at the University of Southampton create a national database to connect amputees with doctors, therapists, and prosthetic suppliers, and he speaks in schools and at medical conferences about his experience and positive attitude. He's even been on a kayaking trip to Greenland with amputees from the British military.[27]

---

27. Kimiko de Freytas-Tamura, "For Quadruple Amputee, Year of Illness 'Was the Most Brilliant,'" *The New York Times*, February 3, 2017, https://www.nytimes.com/2017/02/03/world/europe/alex-lewis-quadruple-amputee.html.

How is it possible to look back on a season of life filled with so much pain and loss with a sense of gratitude? How could anyone see that kind of suffering as a positive thing? The answer lies in one word: *purpose*. When you can see that your suffering has served a purpose in your life, you can be thankful even for the pain.

In this chapter, we'll examine another story of great suffering that served a purpose, the story of Joseph. His dramatic tale of overcoming hardship will inspire you to see that your life—and even your problems—are serving a higher purpose. God has placed you where you are for a purpose. There is a reason for your season. Hold tight to his promises, and you will see his power revealed in the end.

LATCH ON TO THE PROMISE

The story of Joseph is one of the most prominent stories the Old Testament. It comprises thirteen chapters of the book of Genesis, more than a quarter of the book. One reason this story figures so prominently is that it describes a pivotal season in the life of God's people. God had made his covenant with Abraham, who was Joseph's great-grandfather, promising that his descendants would inhabit the land of Canaan, that they would become a numerous people, and that the entire world would be blessed through them. However, God also foretold that the descendants of Abraham would first become slaves in a foreign land: "And he said unto Abram, Know of a surety that thy seed shall be a stranger in a land that is not theirs, and shall serve them; and they shall afflict them four hundred years" (Genesis 15:13). The events in Joseph's life move the descendants of Abraham into Egypt and the time of slavery God had foretold, all according to his purpose.

God's promise is still in effect. In fact, the move of Joseph and his family to Egypt merely positioned them for another part of God's plan. More on that later.

For now, let's look at the idea of promise in the story of Joseph. First, there is the promise that God gave to Abraham and his descendants, which included Joseph. That promise was still operating. And there is another promise in this story, a promise made to Joseph. Through two dreams, God revealed to Joseph that he would someday be in an exalted position and that his brothers would honor him, even though he was one of the youngest in the family (see Genesis 37:5–9). At the very beginning of the story, Joseph understands that his life has a purpose. Not only is he a member of the family that God has chosen to bless the world, but he himself has been singled out to play an important role in that drama. Joseph understands that his life has a purpose. God has promised something special for his life.

Joseph's life took a turn for the worse almost immediately after he received those dreams. Joseph's brothers, who already didn't like him because he seemed to be the favorite of their father, scoffed at the notion that they would somehow serve their little brother. Even their father, Jacob, found the idea hard to believe. Finally, fed up by the favoritism and Joseph's apparent bragging about his future, the older brothers plotted to kill him. Only Reuben, the oldest sibling, intervened to save Joseph's life. Later, the others, still bent on revenge, sold Joseph to merchants in a passing caravan. And so Joseph, the young man whose life held so much promise, was packed off to Egypt as a slave.

However, upon Joseph's arrival in Egypt, we read this: "And the LORD was with Joseph, and he was a prosperous man; and he was in the house of his master the Egyptian" (Genesis 39:2). Joseph's circumstances may have taken a nosedive, but his fortunes rose. How? Why? Because the promise of God was still operating in his life. Joseph's brothers may have despised him, he may have been a slave in a foreign country, but God had not forgotten his promise to this young man. He was able to thrive in circumstances where many other people would have withered because he held on to God's promise.

When you are facing adversity, it's critical to hold tight to the promises of God in your life. As with Joseph, some of those promises are general and some are specific. Some apply to you as a member of the household of faith, and some are given to you personally regarding your life.

In general terms, you have been given the promise of eternal life through faith in Jesus Christ. You, along with all believers in Christ, will inherit eternity. Remember that when your current circumstances seem too much to bear, heaven awaits. That is not pie-in-the-sky promise. It is a secure future that will give you strength and perseverance for each day. You are heir to the promises of God given elsewhere to his children. Remember the blessing of Asher (see Chapter 6). God has promised abundance, favor, wealth, security, and strength. Nothing about your current circumstances affects that promise. God did not forget what he had promised Joseph. Joseph's slavery in Egypt did not negate the promise, and the adversity you face today does not negate God's promises to you. They are as secure as on the day they were given. God never goes back on his Word.

Some of the promises of God are specific, intended for individuals. God revealed to Joseph that he would rise in position above his brothers and that they would someday honor him. That was a promise for Joseph alone. It did not apply to his brothers or any other descendants of Abraham. In the same way, there may be promises God has revealed to you about your future. If so, hold tightly to them. God always honors his Word. How do you recognize the promises of God given to you? You must "test the spirits" (1 John 4:1 NIV). Do not believe every word spoken to you, but put them to the test through prayer and fasting, measuring them against Scripture, the counsel of your pastor, and the wisdom of the church. When you know that God has spoken to you, hold tight to that promise, and do not become discouraged.

The patriarchs—Abraham, Isaac, and Jacob—lived by God's promise, though they had yet to see it fulfilled. Joseph also had to trust God's promises even though his situation seemed to be taking him in a different direction. He demonstrated steadfast faith in God, never losing hope. To rise above adversity, you must do the same. Seek God's blessing in your life. Trust his Word. Hold tight to his purpose for your life. Remember that being faithful to God is always better than seeking comfort for yourself. It's better to be a slave in Egypt and faithful to God's Word than to live like a king but abandon your confidence in God. Trust him; he won't let you down.

UNDERSTAND THE PRINCIPLE OF POSITIONING

Joseph was able to keep his faith in God's promise, and that surely sustained him through the anger and frustration he must have felt at being betrayed by his own brothers. And God was faithful to Joseph even in slavery, causing him to prosper in his role as a slave in the household of a powerful Egyptian official named Potiphar. But Potiphar's house was not Joseph's final destination. He was destined for the great halls of power in the land of

Egypt. So to fulfill his life's purpose, Joseph had to be repositioned yet again. All of this was according to plan. Like a chess master carefully maneuvering his pieces, God carefully and purposely positioned Joseph to fulfill his purpose. Unfortunately, as is often the case in a chess match, that repositioning involved a sacrifice. Joseph was to be betrayed yet again.

Joseph was a handsome young man, and Potiphar's wife became attracted to him. Joseph was far too honorable to take advantage of that situation, and he refused her advances. Angry at his refusal, the woman falsely accused Joseph of rape. That landed Joseph in prison. Even there, however, God blessed Joseph, and he rose to a position of trust, serving as a virtual vice-warden. Also, while in prison, Joseph interpreted a dream for the former cupbearer to Pharaoh, predicting that the man would soon be restored to his position serving the king.

Later, Pharaoh had dreams he could not understand, and the cupbearer remembered Joseph and his ability to interpret dreams. He called for Joseph, who correctly interpreted Pharaoh's dreams, predicting seven years of abundant harvest followed by seven years of famine. Pharaoh was so impressed that he made Joseph his prime minister. Joseph administered all the affairs of the land, answering only to Pharaoh himself. In this lofty position, Joseph was able to ensure that adequate food was stored during the years of abundance to carry the nation through the years of drought.

Let's trace the movement in Joseph's life. He was sold as a slave, which placed him in the land of Egypt. He was falsely accused and sent to prison, which situated him next to the cupbearer to the king. He was then moved into position as prime minister of Egypt, where he had the opportunity to look after the nation's food supply. That put him in a place where he could help his own family, who came to Egypt during the famine to seek food. There was a reason for every season in Joseph's life. Slavery, prison, and even political power: these experiences were meant neither to punish Joseph nor reward him. They were all intended to position him in the right place at the right time to fulfill God's purpose for his life.

As with Joseph, the seasons of your life each have a reason. You are positioned for a purpose. When those seasons come—whether seasons of adversity or of advantage—remember that they are temporary. God will not leave you in the pit; he will bring you out to accomplish his purpose. And if you find yourself particularly blessed, remember that you are blessed to be a blessing. God has given you abundance or favor or wealth so that you can achieve his purpose for your life. Your suffering is not a punishment; it is a preparation for your next placement. Your good fortune is not a paycheck for being faithful; it is a gift that you are to steward for God's purpose. Through good times or bad times, God has a purpose in mind for your life. These seasons are neither final nor fatal. They are stages of preparation as God places you right where he wants you to be.

It may help to remember the analogy of a chess master positioning his or her pieces. A good player will sometimes sacrifice a pawn in order to move a larger piece into advantage. The setback is temporary, a deliberate move to gain advantage. Occasionally a master player will sacrifice a larger piece, like a knight, rook, or even a queen. The master knows that the object of the game is not to preserve all of the pieces. There is no special prize for having sixteen pieces on the board at the end of the game. The object is to capture the king, and any sacrifice that secures that goal is worthwhile. In the same way, God's goal for your life is not to go through without a scratch. He wants you to be holy more than he wants you to be happy. He's willing to sacrifice your short-term comfort to achieve the higher purpose of helping you grow in faith, learn obedience to the Word, cooperate with the Spirit, and fulfill his mission in the world. Any move that advances that purpose is worthwhile, though it may indeed be a painful sacrifice at the time.

What is God's purpose for your life? You may have trouble seeing that sometimes, especially when you're in a season of suffering. But rest assured, God does have a plan in mind for you. He wants you to grow in faith. He wants you to discover and use your spiritual gift. He aims for you to take part in his mission to reach the world for Christ. Keep your eyes on that purpose. That will certainly make it easier to find meaning in your adversity and to make the most of the seasons where you find yourself.

Here is a powerful question that will help you focus on God's future, no matter what your present may be. When you suffer adversity, as Joseph did so many times in his life, ask: "What does this make possible?" So often we focus on what we have lost. We think about the loss of health, loss of finances, loss of friends, or loss of opportunity that come with adversity. Joseph faced losses too—the loss of his family, his reputation, and his freedom. But he didn't dwell on that. He was too busy building for the future. As a slave, he found that he could rise to the position of head of household. As a prisoner, he became the head trustee. What does your setback or problem make possible for you?

If you have lost a job, you are in a position to learn a new skill or change careers. What a possibility! If you have lost money, you are in a position to grow in the area of financial stewardship or to learn how to live with fewer possessions. You might never have moved in that direction. If you have suffered a loss of any kind, it's normal to grieve. But do not dwell in grief indefinitely. At some point, begin to ask yourself, "What is possible for me in this season of life that wasn't possible before now?" By doing so, you'll keep your mind oriented toward God's purpose. Remember, there is a reason for your season. Your current circumstances are just another opportunity to serve God and give him the glory.

TRUST GOD TO PROVIDE

Another key lesson from Joseph's amazing life is that God always provides for his children. We see this time and again in the story of Joseph. When Joseph's jealous brothers were bent on taking his life, God sent Reuben along just in time to intercede for the boy. When Joseph was sold as a slave, "the LORD was with" him (Genesis 39:2). Undoubtedly, Joseph was an expert administrator, but he prospered in Potiphar's house only because of the Lord's blessing. The same was true when Joseph was thrown into prison. Once again, "the LORD was with him; he showed him kindness and granted him favor in the eyes of the prison warden" (Genesis 39:21). All of this was happening so that God could provide for his chosen people during the coming famine. God doesn't have orphans; he takes care of his children.

That's important to remember when you're in a season of adversity. God will provide for you. Part of weathering the stormy season is learning to trust in that provision. Through your season, God is teaching you this truth: "My times are in thy hand" (Psalm 31:15). You can't see all that's happening, but God can. He knows what you need and when you need it. God will allow us to go into precarious positions, but he always provides. And when you learn that lesson in a difficult season, you won't take God's provision for granted. This truth will become precious to you. Every time God moves you to another place in life, you are getting closer to his promise. To become what God has destined you to be, you must allow him to direct your steps into seasons that can't be explained. You must trust him to provide, even when you don't see how that's possible.

We see this principle played out in the life of Jesus. After his baptism he was led into the wilderness "by the Spirit" to be tempted (Matthew 4:1). Though he faced extreme hunger after fasting for forty days, he refused to give in to the temptation to make bread from stone. He trusted the Father to provide for his needs. When Jesus was traveling from Judea to Galilee, Scripture says that "he must needs go through Samaria" (John 4:4), even though that was a detour from the usual route. He trusted the Father through that detour, and it yielded an encounter with a Samaritan woman that led to the salvation of an entire village.

Trust God to provide during every season of your life. While he is positioning you for the promise, he's also positioning the promise for you. God never promises what he has not already provided. When God spoke to Abraham, he said, "For a father of many nations have I made thee" (Genesis 17:5). He spoke of those things that were not as though they already were. For in God's sight and in God's Word, they were so. When you are in a season of adversity, setback, rejection, or suffering, know that God's promises to you are secure. Trust him to provide for you during your season of struggle. He will not abandon you.

SEE GOD'S POWER DISPLAYED

A favorite event in the Joseph story is when he reveals his identity to his brothers. They had come to Egypt seeking grain because there was a severe famine throughout the region. Joseph, of course, was now a powerful official in Egypt, and it was to him that they made their request for food. Not surprisingly, they didn't recognize their long-lost brother. They would never have dreamed that he could be in such a position, having been sold as a slave. And Joseph looked every bit the part of an Egyptian lord. He spoke the Egyptian language and was undoubtedly dressed in the finest Egyptian clothing. The brothers had no idea that the man they bowed down before was their own brother. And there it was—the fulfillment of Joseph's dreams, given to him so many years before. At long last, his brothers gave him honor, and he was in an exalted position over them. God's power was now fully on display. The promise given to Joseph had been fulfilled. What's more, the whole plan was now obvious: God had positioned Joseph where he was in order to save the lives of his own family. Incredible!

A lesser man would have thought of revenge or at least of gloating at the reversal of fortune, but Joseph had no such thought. He had learned the lesson of positioning. He understood that all of this had been according to God's plan. When he finally revealed his identity to his brothers, he was so overcome with emotion that he ordered everyone else out of the room and broke down in tears (Genesis 45:1–2). At last, he said, "I am Joseph; doth my father yet live?" (Genesis 45:3). His greatest concern was to be reunited with his aging father.

The brothers, however, were too afraid to speak. They knew full well that they had dealt treacherously with this man, who now held the power of life or death over them. They were terrified! But Joseph had no thought of getting even. He said, "I am your brother Joseph, the one you sold into Egypt! And now, do not be distressed and do not be angry with yourselves for selling me here, because it was to save lives that God sent me ahead of you. For two years now there has been famine in the land, and for the next five years there will be no plowing and reaping. But God sent me ahead of you to preserve for you a remnant on earth and to save your lives by a great deliverance. So then, it was not you who sent me here, but God" (Genesis 45:4–8 NIV).

The power of God was obvious to Joseph. He understood that he had been positioned for a purpose. And God had indeed honored his promises, every single one. He had provided for Joseph through every season of his life. And now the purpose of sufferings was revealed to all: it was to save many lives.

When God brings you out of your season of adversity, his purpose will finally be made clear to you. You may catch glimpses of it now, or you may know the purpose but have to wait patiently for it to be revealed. Other people may not understand what's happening in your life. Some of them may mock you or even oppose you. Be patient. Don't lose hope. And don't become angry or vindictive. Remember that God has positioned you for a purpose. Wait for his power to be displayed and for your purpose to be revealed.

When that happens, your response will indicate whether or not you learned the lessons of adversity. Some folk see God's power displayed but return immediately to being vindictive, petty, or having a bad attitude toward others. Though they claim the blessing of God's forgiveness, they refuse to forgive others. That is foolish, and only makes them miss out on further blessings. As Paul wrote, "The heir, as long as he is a child, differeth nothing from a servant, though he be lord of all" (Galatians 4:1). If you emerge from your season of adversity with the same mindset and attitude that you took into it, you might as well still be suffering because God's work has had no effect on you. Yet when you truly see his power on display, positioning you, providing for you, and fulfilling his purpose in you, it will change how you think and how you behave toward others.

What did you learn at Potiphar's house? What were your take-aways from your experience of adversity? Have you learned to be lied to or slandered without losing your faith—or your cool? Have you learned how to deal with strife and envy without letting it affect your spirit? Sometimes, rather than seeing the power of God through our adversity, we see only how it affects us person-ally. Rather than learning from God's power and purpose, we sim-ply become more like our negative experience. Don't allow that to happen to you.

Focus on the power of God displayed in you and through you, not on the negativity of your circumstances, of other people, or of the world in general. You can go through a hard time, but don't let it harden your spirit. You can be out in the cold without becoming coldhearted. Joseph was able to focus on what God was doing—on how his power was on display in and through the seasons of suffering. You can do the same. When you emerge from your troubles, give glory to God for what he has done. Then look for ways that you can bless others who are facing tough seasons of their own. Overcome the pit; don't let the pit overcome you.

REST IN THE PURPOSE

You are where you are for a reason. The adversity you suffer in no way negates the promise of God in your life. He has a purpose for you and though it may be hard to see at first, the season you are in is positioning you to carry out that purpose.

What season are you in right now? Is it a season of loss, setback, suffering? Don't allow yourself to wallow in despair. Ask, "What does this season make possible?" Asking that question will reveal clues to your purpose, making you better able to withstand the difficulties you now face. God has a reason for your season.

Are you in a season of advantage? Remember that it is God's power that brought you here. Don't lord it over those who contributed to your difficulties or who failed to help you when you were down. They were part of God's plan. Your purpose will always be to use God's power to benefit others. Joseph was positioned as he was to save many lives, not to say, "I told you so!" Let your attitude be laced with humility because you realize that God is responsible for whatever advantages you enjoy. This season also has a purpose. There is a reason why you are blessed. It is to be a blessing.

God's promises to you are true and they are secure. He is positioning you for a purpose. He will provide for you, no matter the difficulties you face. And when you see his power displayed, you will have the opportunity to help others on their journey. There is a reason for your season. Trust God and you will see his power revealed.

THE SUCCESSFUL SEVEN

- List the general promises God has made to you as a believer in Christ. Circle those that provide the most assurance for the season you now face.

- If God has revealed a specific promise to you, test that promise against Scripture and the counsel of a mature believer.

- Create a timeline of your life, marking each time God has repositioned you. Show the timeline to a trusted friend and discuss your life's purpose.

- Name the one thing you most need from the Lord in order to weather your current season, then ask him to provide.

- Name three lessons you have learned from your current season, and share one lesson with a friend.

- Ask a friend or mentor this question: "Do you see any ingratitude in my life?" Ask them to hold you accountable for a humble attitude.

- Memorize Ecclesiastes 3:1.

10
Blessing Others

Do nothing out of selfish ambition or vain conceit. Rather, in humility value others above yourselves, not looking to your own interests but each of you to the interests of the others.
—Philippians 2:3–4 NIV

THE WINNING ATTITUDE

I gain by giving to others.

SEEDS OF HOPE

War may be the ultimate form of adversity. During wartime people are often forced to make difficult choices. For some, this hardship turns them inward. They choose to cope with their difficulties by thinking only of themselves and their survival. For others, the horror of war has a way of turning them outward. They are able to look beyond their own condition to see the needs of others. Some are willing to risk their own comfort or security to procure the survival of those around them. Such was the case with a group of botanists who were tasked with guarding, of all things, a seed warehouse during the siege of Leningrad. The siege began on September 8, 1941, when Hitler's armies cut off the last road into Leningrad, now called Saint Petersburg, the second-largest city in Russia. The siege was not lifted until January 27, 1944, lasting 842 days. During those brutal months, the people suffered extreme hunger, especially during the viciously cold winter of 1941–42. By January, temperatures had plunged to 26 degrees below zero and some 100,000 people per month were starving to death.[28] Those who remained alive became increasingly desperate. Murders for food or ration cards were commonplace, and there were confirmed reports of cannibalism within the city.[29]

During that terrible winter, a small group of botanists had charge of a seed bank. Their mission was to preserve the seeds for future generations of the Soviet people. The collection included some 40,000 types of food plants, including rice, wheat, corn, peas, and some 6,000 varieties of potatoes. These researchers at the Vavilov Institute of Plant Industry held in trust one of the largest repositories of crop seeds in the world, an incredible supply of diverse genetic material. It was also an incredible supply of food, amounting to several tons of edible substances. These scientists worked day and night to protect the seeds from thieves, from the cold, from rodents, from every imaginable threat. The future of their country depended upon it.

Of course, these researchers also were starving to death, just like everyone else. Yet they realized that if they succumbed to the temptation to eat the seed stores, millions more might starve in

---

28. Ann Reid, *Leningrad: Tragedy of a City Under Siege, 1941–44* (New York: Walker Publishing Company, Inc., 2011), 3.
29. Ibid., 290–91. *SunSentinel* http://articles.sun-sentinel.com/1992-05-13/news/9202080144_1_vavilov-institute-food-crops-leningrad.

the future. They took turns standing guard around the clock, never allowing anyone to be alone with the food. Then one cold January day, A. G. Stchukin, a specialist in groundnuts, died at his writing table. D. S. Ivanov, a rice specialist, passed away soon after. Later, coworkers found several thousand packs of rice in his collection, food he had preserved for future generations even as he weakened and died from hunger. In all, nine scientists starved to death because they refused to deplete the priceless gene bank for their own benefit. Outside the Institute, some Leningraders were killing one another for scraps of food, yet these selfless souls refused to eat at the expense of others, even those yet to be born.[30]

The humble sacrifice of those dedicated scientists illustrates an important principle about dealing with adversity. No matter what form of trouble you may face, it is vital to preserve your personal integrity. In good times and in bad, remember that you have not been placed on this earth for yourself alone. You are here for others. Perhaps no biblical character embodies that principle so well as Hadassah, a young Jewish girl living in exile who rose to a position of great privilege, wealth, and power. Yet when a crisis came, she had the poise to remember her purpose and risk everything to win the protection of others. We know her as Esther, and her story will inspire you to remain true to yourself and your purpose, regardless of what you suffer.

YOUR PURPOSE IS NOT YOUR OWN

Esther began life with the name Hadassah, a lowly Jewish girl living in exile in Persia. Hadassah was an orphan and was raised by her cousin Mordecai. Xerxes, the powerful king of Persia, had a falling out with his queen, Vashti, because she defied him public-

---

30. S. M. Alexanyan and V. I. Krivchenko, "Vavilov Institute scientists heroically preserve world plant genetic resources collection during siege of Leningrad," *Diversity* 7, no. 4 (1991):10–12.

ly. After deposing Vashti from her position, Xerxes began a search for a new queen by holding a beauty contest. Mordecai, realizing that this was a great opportunity for his beautiful young cousin, entered Hadassah in the contest. However, he insisted that she use her Persian name, Esther, concealing her ethnic background or family ties. So Esther was taken to the royal court along with a host of other women for a year of beauty treatments before being presented to the king. Meanwhile, Mordecai stayed near the entrance of the courtyard to keep tabs on how Esther was doing. Esther immediately became popular with everyone she met, and when her turn came to meet the king, it was love at first sight. Esther became the new queen of Persia!

This is a rags-to-riches story about a charming young girl who rose to a position of great fame and wealth. It's the happy ending of everyone's dreams. Just be yourself, do the right things, and you will find fortune beyond your wildest dreams. However, that's not the end of the story.

Haman, one of the king's ministers, took an intense dislike to Mordecai because Mordecai refused to bow down to Haman in public. Haman was so incensed that he hatched a plot to have all Jews in the Persian Empire put to death. He actually succeeded in passing a law saying that on a certain day, anyone could kill Jewish people without penalty and seize their property. The king, not realizing that his own wife was Jewish, approved the law.

That's when Mordecai sprang into action. He sent a message to Esther, calling on her to go to the king and beg for justice on behalf of her people. Esther balked at the request because it was a dangerous move. It was forbidden to enter the king's presence without an invitation—and Esther had not been called to see the king for over a month. Showing up uninvited could cost Esther

her life. She demurred. Mordecai, however, was resolute. He sent another message to Esther, saying, "Do not think that because you are in the king's house you alone of all the Jews will escape. For if you remain silent at this time, relief and deliverance for the Jews will arise from another place, but you and your father's family will perish. And who knows but that you have come to your royal position for such a time as this?" (Esther 4:13–14 NIV).

Mordecai understood one of the first principles of being a child of God. Your life is not your own; it belongs to him. Mordecai knew that whether his niece was living humbly as Hadassah, a Jewish refugee, or living lavishly as Esther, favored wife of the emperor, the purpose of her life was to serve the Lord's purpose, not her own. She had been placed in a position of great privilege, but that was not for her benefit alone. She was there on behalf of others. Esther began life at the bottom, and she was elevated to the top. In either status, her life had one purpose: to serve God by serving others.

The same is true for you. This concept of being placed where you are "for such a time as this" runs throughout Scripture and applies to everyone from kings and queens to ordinary citizens. When Moses went to confront Pharaoh, telling him to release God's people from slavery, God instructed Moses to tell Pharaoh this: "But I have raised you up for this very purpose, that I might show you my power and that my name might be proclaimed in all the earth" (Exodus 9:16 NIV). Imagine that! God put *Pharaoh* in his position merely to accomplish God's purpose.

The same is true for us in that, regardless of our station, God is working his plan through us. Paul wrote, "Therefore, my dear friends, as you have always obeyed—not only in my presence, but now much more in my absence—continue to work out your salvation with fear and trembling, for it is God who works in you to will and to act in order to fulfill his good purpose" (Philippians 2:12–13 NIV). And he told Timothy, "Who hath saved us, and called us with an holy calling, not according to our works, but according to his own purpose and grace, which was given us in Christ Jesus before the world began" (2 Timothy 1:9).

Do not think for a moment that the grace God has showered into your life has been for your benefit only. The very fact that God has saved you indicates that he is at work in your life. This isn't because of anything you've done but in order to fulfill God's purpose through you. Paul made that idea even more explicit when writing to the church at Corinth. He said, "What? know ye not that your body is the temple of the Holy Ghost which is in you, which ye have of God, and ye are not your own? For ye are bought with a price: therefore glorify God in your body, and in your spirit, which are God's" (1 Corinthians 6:19–20). Having saved you, God has a claim on your life. You are not your own; you belong to him. Your purpose now is to do his will, whatever that may entail.

And, as Mordecai reminded Esther, don't think that you can somehow circumvent God's purpose and still enjoy the blessings he's provided. You are where you are for a purpose, God's purpose. As the Proverbs say, "Many are the plans in a person's heart, but it is the LORD's purpose that prevails" (Proverbs 19:21 NIV). God's will *shall* be done in the world, with or without you. Wouldn't it be better to take part?

When you are facing adversity, it can be hard to see God's purpose. One reason we fail to see what God is doing is that we think only about ourselves. The devil would like nothing better than to keep your mind focused on your problems. When you are consumed with thoughts about your finances, your loneliness, or your pain, you have no vision for other people. You cannot see how they too may be suffering. You miss the connection between your gifts and resources and the needs of others. Saying, "Me first," will prevent you from seeing the bigger picture.

If it is difficult to see God's purpose when facing adversity, it can be even harder when things are going well. Adversity focuses our attention on our own needs, and prosperity focuses our attention on our own desires. Either way, we're focused on ourselves. And when we are self-focused, we are useless to God and his purpose. When you are consumed with having money or luxury for yourself, you'll be oblivious to the suffering of others. When you enjoy good health, it can be difficult to remember those who suffer chronic pain or can't afford to visit the doctor. Though the Bible makes it clear that it's no sin to be wealthy, many wealthy people fall into sin by developing a selfish and uncaring attitude toward those in need.

Regardless of whether you are now facing adversity or have risen above it, remember that your life is not your own. You are here for a reason, and that reason is to serve God by serving others. Look around you. What needs do you see? What resources do you have—financially, relationally, spiritually? What might you do to bring the love of God and the message of salvation to those who need it most? Look to benefit others, not yourself. Who knows? Perhaps you were placed where you are for such a time as this.

DON'T SACRIFICE YOUR PRINCIPLES

The challenge placed before Esther was a test of her character. She had come from humble beginnings but risen to a position of great wealth and comfort. How far would she go to maintain that comfortable life? Up to this point, she had successfully concealed her identity. Would she now deny that heritage altogether? Would this threat to her safety lead Esther to abandon her upbringing, her family, and her faith? She faced a difficult choice, and we face a similar choice more often than we may realize.

The word *stress* indicates a tension between two forces. When you feel stress, it is usually because circumstances are pushing you beyond your limits in some area—physical, emotional, spiritual, or financial. For example, when you have bills you can't pay, you feel financial stress. You have an obligation to your creditor, but also to your family and your own integrity. There is tension between what you would like to do and what you feel able to do. Some choose to relieve that stress by sacrificing their character. They may lie, cheat on taxes or on welfare regulations, or even steal. They resolve the tension by sacrificing their principles. It's remarkably easy to do.

Others face stress in relationships when, for example, they do not feel loved or fulfilled in a marriage. They want to be faithful to their wedding vow, but they also feel lonely or abandoned. There is tension between their needs and the commitments they have made. Here, too, some choose to relieve that stress by sacrificing their principles, looking for fulfillment outside the bonds of their marriage. They resolve the tension by denying who they are.

When you face adversity of any kind, you will likely be faced with a similar test of character. Will you lie in order to get ahead of a rival at work? Will you gossip or spread rumors to get back at someone who has wronged you? Will you withhold your tithes from God or your offerings from the poor in order to provide comforts for yourself? Will you violate your conscience in an attempt to secure the life you think you deserve? This was the question facing Esther, and it's one you may be facing right now.

Esther refused to sacrifice her principles for her own protec-tion. She would not deny her identity as a child of God to avoid risk or adversity. She chose character over comfort. From the way she put that decision into action, we can learn four important les-sons on how to respond with integrity.

The first thing we notice about Esther's response is that she quickly and immediately chose to put others ahead of herself. When she received the second message from Haman, she re-sponded without hesitation: "Go, gather together all the Jews who are in Susa, and fast for me. Do not eat or drink for three days, night or day. I and my attendants will fast as you do. When this is done, I will go to the king, even though it is against the law. And if I perish, I perish" (Esther 4:16 NIV). Esther chose to put the welfare of others ahead of herself.

Next, we notice that Esther relied on God for her strength and protection. Interestingly, the name of God is not mentioned anywhere in the story of Esther. Yet Esther clearly depended on God in her time of trouble. She asked others to fast on her behalf and she fasted too. Fasting is not a popular practice today, which may indicate how much we favor our own comfort over devotion to the Lord. Throughout history, fasting has been a way for God's people to focus their minds and hearts on him and the practice is closely linked with prayer. Esther understood that she must align herself with God's will and seek his help in order to prevail in her mission to save her people.

Third, we see that Esther was willing to do the right thing for her people even though it was against the law of the land. She understood that faithfulness to the will of God is a higher priority than complicity with human authority. As Christians, we know that we must obey the law and cooperate with civil authorities whenever possible. Paul urged this in no uncertain terms in his letter to the church in Rome: "Let everyone be subject to the governing authorities, for there is no authority except that which God has established. The authorities that exist have been established by God. Consequently, whoever rebels against the authority is rebelling against what God has instituted, and those who do so will bring judgment on themselves" (Romans 13:1–2 NIV). However, Paul was speaking about good civil authorities that were doing the Lord's will by ensuring justice for all. Throughout history, and based in part on Esther's example, Christians have understood that their allegiance to God must take precedence over allegiance to a civil government that has abandoned its rightful purpose.

Esther could have hidden behind the law as a way of excusing herself from taking action. She could have maintained her comfortable position while saying, "I don't have a choice." But she refused to deny her identity as a child of God. She put God's will ahead of her allegiance to the country in which she lived.

Fourth, we see that Esther maintained her character by refusing to fight against Haman on his terms. He had resorted to treachery in order to attack the Jews—all based on his grudge against Mordecai. Esther, however, would not engage in the same methods. She conducted herself in a proper way, even though the situation was grave. She did indeed go to the king, and he received her gladly. That might have been an opportunity to viciously attack Haman, but Esther showed restraint. She asked the king to invite Haman to dinner. As the story played out over the following days, Haman dined with Esther and the king on two occasions. It was not until the second occasion, when Esther was sure that the king was well-disposed to hear her plea, that Esther revealed the truth about herself, her people, and Haman's plot. True to form, Haman confirmed his low character in the king's presence by trying to strong arm Esther.

Esther did not fight fire with fire. She maintained her integrity and her dignity, meeting the plots hatched by the ruthless Haman with quiet confidence in the truth. Esther succeeded because she refused to sacrifice her principles. It will always be tempting to believe that the depth of your suffering justifies any and every attempt to escape it. That is never the case. Remain true to your identity as a child of God. Do not use the evil deeds of others as an excuse to engage in evil yourself. Do not sacrifice your principles for your progress. If you do, you will lose both in the end. Hold onto your integrity and you will see God's deliverance.

ENJOY GOD'S PROTECTION

The end of Esther's story is a joyous one. When the king learned the truth about Haman's intentions, he was furious. The evil Haman was hanged on a gallows he had constructed specifically for Mordecai. Though the king could not legally change the order he had given that Jews could be killed, he issued another order saying that they had the right to defend themselves, which forestalled any attacks on God's people. By placing Esther in her position of influence and protecting her as she made her request of the king, God had once again come to the rescue of his people. Esther's courage, bravery, and integrity had paid off. Because she was willing to put others ahead of herself, both she and her people were saved.

It should be no surprise that God defends those who maintain the integrity of their faith in him because the Scriptures often make that same point. Solomon wrote, "Whoso walketh uprightly shall be saved: but he that is perverse in his ways shall fall at once" (Proverbs 28:18), and "For the upright shall dwell in the land, and the perfect shall remain in it" (Proverbs 2:21), and, "The integrity of the upright shall guide them: but the perverseness of transgressors shall destroy them" (Proverbs 11:3). For those who suffer any kind of adversity, keeping the faith is the best course of action—and the only one that will lead to deliverance. Those who plot and scheme their way out of negative circumstances only make matters worse.

The apostle Paul commented on the righteous life this way: "But have renounced the hidden things of dishonesty, not walking in craftiness, nor handling the word of God deceitfully; but by manifestation of the truth commending ourselves to every man's conscience in the sight of God" (2 Corinthians 4:2). When we honor our conscience, doing what is right in every circumstance, we can have confidence in approaching God. When we sacrifice our principles or our faith, we lose. James wrote, "If any of you lack wisdom, let him ask of God, that giveth to all men liberally, and upbraideth not; and it shall be given him. But let him ask in faith, nothing wavering. For he that wavereth is like a wave of the sea driven with the wind and tossed. For let not that man think that he shall receive any thing of the Lord" (James 1:5–7). When you are double-minded, wanting to please God but also wanting to please yourself, your prayers will have no power. When you stand firm in your faith, not wavering in your identity as a child of God, you will receive your answer.

Trust God, do the right thing, and you will see his protection revealed. Esther was certainly not the only Bible hero to discover that. Moses was adopted into the household of Pharaoh, a place he could have stayed indefinitely, enjoying the comforts of wealth and privilege. But he "refused to be called the son of Pharaoh's daughter; Choosing rather to suffer affliction with the people of God, than to enjoy the pleasures of sin for a season" (Hebrews 11:24–25).

Daniel, like Esther, enjoyed a position of great privilege but was forced to make a character choice when his king passed a law forbidding prayer to God. Understanding full well the consequences of breaking that law, Daniel "went into his house; and his windows being open in his chamber toward Jerusalem, he kneeled upon his knees three times a day, and prayed, and gave thanks before his God, as he did aforetime" (Daniel 6:10). When Daniel was thrown to the lions as punishment, God protected him.

Shadrach, Meshach, and Abednego were threatened with death if they refused to bow down and worship an idol. They said, "If it be so, our God whom we serve is able to deliver us from the burning fiery furnace, and he will deliver us out of thine hand, O king. But if not, be it known unto thee, O king, that we will not serve thy gods, nor worship the golden image which thou hast set up" (Daniel 3:17–18). God did indeed protect them, and they came through the fire unharmed.

In each case, these godly people had the opportunity to preserve their own comfort and escape adversity—even death—at the expense of their integrity. They refused, knowing that God would deliver them if they were obedient to him. There is nothing to be gained by sacrificing your principles, fudging on your faith, and putting your own well-being ahead of God's will or of doing what's right for others. On the contrary, when we maintain faith in the face of hard times, we have an opportunity to see God's power revealed.

TRUST AND OBEY

From an overcomer's standpoint, the key to Esther's success was her ability to trust God and move forward. If she had believed that everything she attained was for herself, she wouldn't have risked so much. And if she had been unwilling to trust in God's protection, she couldn't have done it. She needed to keep her poise and be ready to act when the time came. The temptation for those trying to move beyond any adversity is to see their progress as theirs alone. It isn't. Everything you're experiencing—and all the blessings you will receive—are for others. Do not be afraid to risk the progress you have made when God calls you to be faithful. Trust God and keep moving.

No matter where you are today, you are not there by accident. If you are in the king's palace, so to speak, enjoying a position of privilege as Esther did, remember that it's not for you alone. God has placed you there for a reason. Do not hoard the position, privilege, or provision for yourself. Look for opportunities to advance God's work and to do good for others.

And if you are facing the trial of your life, don't be afraid to put your principles ahead of your own comfort. God rewards those who are faithful to him during times of adversity. Remember your identity as a child of God and remember your calling. Be true to yourself and to the will of the Lord. That's when you will see his power revealed. You are not the only character in the story God is writing with your life. You are here for others. Bless them, and you too will be blessed.

———◇———

THE SUCCESSFUL SEVEN

- List the people in your life toward whom you have some responsibility (examples might be your family members, friends, neighbors). Pray that you will have the fortitude to put their needs first.

- Name the greatest privilege you now enjoy. State how you can use that advantage as a resource to bless others.

- Esther was placed in the palace for "such a time as this." State the challenge or opportunity for which God uniquely positioned you.

- In what area are you tempted to compromise your integrity to avoid some difficulty? Ask a friend to hold you accountable in that area.

- Name the thing in your life that you fear losing the most, then offer it to God.

- Recommit yourself to being faithful to God in all situations.

- Memorize Philippians 2:3-4

◇

11
Asking the Right Questions

Get wisdom. Though it cost all you have, get understanding.
—Proverbs 4:7 NIV

THE WINNING ATTITUDE

I grow stronger through hard times.

A FRESH PERSPECTIVE

When it comes to beating adversity, few people have a more deserved reputation for overcoming than does Helen Keller, the deaf and blind girl who went on to graduate from college and become a prolific author and advocate for women's rights and other causes. Keller was born in rural Alabama in 1880 and had the ability to see and hear, but she lost both after a severe, but undiagnosed illness when she was just nineteen months old. Many people are familiar with her amazing achievements as described in the stage and film production *The Miracle Worker* and in Keller's autobiography, *The Story of My Life*. Many also know about Anne Sullivan, Helen Keller's teacher and companion who taught Helen how to communicate. What they may not know is the amazing breakthrough that led Helen Keller to discover language.

Anne Sullivan arrived in the Keller household as a teacher when Helen was just six years old. Unable to see, hear, or speak, the child lived an isolated, almost feral life. She would take food from other people's plates and eat with her hands and had no concept of language. There was little way to teach her anything, let alone manners. Anne Sullivan moved Helen to a cabin to work on both her table manners and her ability to communicate. Anne began instructing Helen by using finger signs for various words, such as *doll* and *mug*. Helen could mimic the signs but was frustrated because she could not connect the symbols to specific objects. Anne had made many attempts to show Helen that the word *doll* could apply to both her rag doll and her porcelain doll, and that *water* was not the same as *mug*, which held the water, but Helen simply could not understand. Ironically, *water* was the one word that she later remembered hearing and saying before the illness robbed her of sight and hearing.

One day, in a fit of anger, Helen tossed her porcelain doll to the floor, shattering it. She simply could not comprehend that d-o-l-l was a word, much less that it represented the toy she had held. Helen could make letter symbols with her hands, but had no idea what they meant. She lived in a world of darkness with no way to express her thoughts, even in her own mind.

The breakthrough came later that day when Anne took Helen outside to the hand-operated well. Someone was pumping water, and Anne had the idea of putting Helen's hand under the spout. With the water flowing, Anne signed w-a-t-e-r so that Helen could feel both the water and the hand symbols. Helen describes what happened next: "I stood still, my whole attention fixed upon the motions of the fingers. Suddenly I felt a misty consciousness as of something forgotten—a thrill of returning thought; and somehow the mystery of language was revealed to me. I knew that 'w-a-t-e-r' meant the wonderful cool something that was flowing over my hand. That living word awakened my soul, gave it light, hope, joy, set it free!"[31]

Sometimes the key to solving a difficult problem is to vary your approach. When you see the situation from a new perspective, a breakthrough often comes. Also, Anne Sullivan was right in believing that education was the key to changing Helen Keller's life. Learning revolutionized Helen's life and enabled her to overcome adversity that would cripple many people. The big change happened when Anne Sullivan began to look at the problem of communication in a new way.

Learning is always a key to overcoming adversity. Whether your problem is physical blindness, spiritual blindness, illness, debt, divorce, or any of the many problems that we face, you will not move beyond it until you learn the lessons it has to offer. One biblical character stands out as a prime example of learning from adversity. Like the young Helen Keller, this man at first had a difficult time grasping the lessons in his situation. His mind got stuck in his suffering, asking God the same question over and over again. He needed a new perspective, a new way of looking at his problems, and God provided that new perspective in a dramatic fashion. The man's name is Job, and he has become a symbol of

---

31   . Helen Keller, *The Story of My Life*, (Garden City, NJ: Doubleday, Page & Company, 1921), 22–23.

undeserved suffering, and of faith in enduring it. As we examine his story, you will see the power of asking the right questions in order to learn from your circumstances and overcome the challenges you face.

THE WRONG QUESTIONS

Three books of the Bible deal almost exclusively with adversity and how to respond to it in order to advance. Psalms is an *emotional response* to adversity; it shows the range of pain and praise that we experience through hard times and helps us express those thoughts. Proverbs is a *practical response* to adversity; its pithy sayings give us practical guidelines for applying God's wisdom to our lives. And the book of Job is an *intellectual response* to adversity; it explains that bad things do indeed happen to good people and teaches us to respond with faith.

Job is legendary as an example of patient suffering. If you're not familiar with the story, you can review the basic outline in Job chapters 1 and 2. Job was a righteous man who lived a blameless life. One day Satan suggested to God that the only reason Job worshiped God was that Job's life was so perfect. Satan wagered that if God were to allow Job's wealth and his family to be taken from him, he would curse God. Then God allowed great evil to befall Job, destroying his wealth and family. His faith did not waver. Instead, Job "fell to the ground in worship and said: 'Naked I came from my mother's womb, and naked I will depart. The Lord gave and the Lord has taken away; may the name of the Lord be praised.' In all this, Job did not sin by charging God with wrongdoing" (Job 1:20–22 NIV). What an amazing display of faith!

Later Satan argued that Job was faithful only because he himself had not been harmed. So in a second round of adversity, God gave permission for Satan to afflict Job with painful sores all over his body. Even then, suffering great physical pain, Job remained faithful. He remains a stunning example of faith in the face of suffering.

There's a bit more to the story, however. Job first began to feel sorry for himself, wishing he'd never been born. Then he wondered why all of this trouble happened to him. That's a progression of thought we've probably all had at some time. "I wish I were dead" followed by "Why me, Lord?" Most of the book of Job is a series of dialogues between Job and four of his friends who came to "comfort" him. Through the exchanges between Job, his wife, and his friends, we see several points of view displayed. It seems that everyone had a question about Job and his situation.

First, Job's wife asked, "Are you still maintaining your integrity? Curse God and die" (Job 2:9 NIV). Her opinion was that faith was no longer any use to Job in his suffering, and that he might as well be dead. She's asking something like, "What good is God?"

Second, Job's friends took turns advancing the idea that Job must have done something wrong to deserve his suffering. One of them asked Job, "...Who ever perished, being innocent?..." (Job 4:7). They hammer Job with this idea that God is always fair and would not allow an innocent person to suffer. Therefore, Job must have done something wrong. They tell him to repent so he can get over his illness. Their question sounds something like one we often ask, "What did I do to deserve this?"

A third question comes from Job himself. We read it in Job 10:3 (NIV): "Does it please you to oppress me, to spurn the work of your hands, while you smile on the plans of the wicked?" Job is taking God to task because Job believes his suffering to be unfair. Job argues that wicked people seem to be doing fine, but God seems to be punishing him. Why? That's a question we all ask in one form or another. It usually sounds something like, "Why is God doing this to me?" or "Why is life so unfair?"

Job asks another, more haunting question a few verses later, saying, "Why then did you bring me out of the womb? I wish I had died before any eye saw me. If only I had never come into being, or had been carried straight from the womb to the grave!" (Job 10:18–19 NIV). Suffering makes us wonder similar things. "What's the point of living?" we may wonder.

A final question from Job has to do with the outlook for the future. Is there any hope? Is this all my life will be? The question Job asked may sound hopeful to us, given our perspective from this side of Easter: "If a man die, shall he live again?" (Job 14:14). You and I know that the answer is yes. Thanks to Jesus' resurrection from the dead, we do indeed have hope of an eternal life. But remember that Job had no such knowledge. He lived long before the miracle of the resurrection. From his vantage point, the question sounds more like this: "Is this all there is to my life?" Everyone who had suffered adversity has probably wondered the same. Suffering changes our reality. The world looks different to us now than it did before. From that perspective, we wonder if things will ever improve.

The questions we find in Job's story are the same basic questions we all face when we suffer.

- What good is God?

- What did I do to deserve this?

- Why is God doing this to me?

- What's the point of living?
- Is this all there is for me?

They seem like good questions. So what is the answer?

THE RIGHT QUESTIONS

Interestingly, those questions are never answered directly in the book of Job. Though each one represents a typical response to suffering, this book of the Bible does not directly say, "Here's why you are suffering" or "Here's the point of living." Instead, God shows up at the end of the book to ask a few questions of his own. Clearly impatient both with Job's friends and with Job himself, God spoke to Job out of a whirlwind, asking some tough questions in response to Job's charge that God had been unfair with him. God asked—

- "Who is this that obscures my plans with words without knowledge?" (Job 38:2 NIV).
- "Where were you when I laid the earth's foundation?" (Job 38:4 NIV).
- "Have you ever given orders to the morning or shown the dawn its place?" (Job 38:12 NIV).
- "Where does darkness reside?" (Job 38:19 NIV).
- "Can you loosen Orion's belt" (Job 38:31 NIV).
- "Will the one who contends with the Almighty correct him? Let him who accuses God answer him!" (Job 40:2, NIV).

The barrage of questions continued for three chapters until Job finally had enough. The point, of course, is that God's wisdom is far superior to Job's; therefore, Job had no ability to question the things God did or didn't do. God is God, and Job isn't. Job got the point. At length, Job answered God with yet another question, a better one than those he'd asked before: "I am unworthy—how can I reply to you?" (Job 40:4 NIV).

Job finally realized that he'd been asking the wrong questions. Rather than focusing on himself, wondering why he was suffering, wondering why God was treating him unfairly, wondering what would become of his life, Job should have thinking about the character of God. Later, Job said, "My ears had heard of you but now my eyes have seen you. Therefore I despise myself and repent in dust and ashes" (Job 42:6 NIV). Humility, not hubris, is the best posture for learning. When Job was able to put aside his self-righteous sense of entitlement and to focus on God, he grew a lot. Job needed a change of perspective, and God provided that in a most dramatic fashion.

We often need a change of perspective in order to grow. Adversity tends to drive us inward, making us think mostly about ourselves. That self-absorption can slip into self-pity and feeling sorry for yourself is a sure way to remain stuck in your rut. When you feel pathetic, entitled, indignant, or angry with God, you will never learn from your circumstances. To make progress, you, like Anne Sullivan trying to teach Helen Keller, must approach your problems in a new way. You need a change of perspective. One way to do that is to start asking different questions.

QUESTIONS THAT OVERCOME

Let's review the questions we find in Job's story, probably the same questions you are asking about your circumstances and replace them with better ones. Here are five things to ask during adversity that will help you grow. Ask them honestly and openly, and you'll find wisdom to overcome the challenges you face.

1. WHAT IS GOD TEACHING ME?

Our first question we ask during adversity is usually some version of "Why is God doing this to me?" You may wonder why you've been singled out, so it seems, by God. Is he angry with you? Have you done something wrong? Or is God simply unfair? That's a conclusion many people make.

Those are natural questions, and when we ask them we are at least taking our struggles to the right place. As the story of Job clearly shows, God is in control. He could have prevented Job's suffering, but he didn't. He knew about it in advance and he allowed it to happen. The same must be true for our circumstances. And because we know that God is in control, we may wonder about his character, which is the thought that underlies these questions.

It's important to remember that God did not inflict Job's suffering but he did allow it. That distinction is important. It doesn't mean that God specifically intends for people to suffer, only that he allows suffering to exist in the world. Bad things happen for lots of reasons—because of sin in the world, sin in other people, our own foolish actions, and even demonic activity, as was the case with Job. When you suffer, God hasn't singled you out for punishment. He's simply allowing the consequences of sin to play out in our world.

As to the question of fairness, the writer of Psalm 73 wondered about the same thing. Seeing that people who reject God often live comfortable lives while the righteous suffer, he was bothered by the seeming unfairness of it all. He was so discouraged by this that he nearly lost faith—until he caught a glimpse of God. The psalmist wrote, "When I thought to know this, it was too painful for me; Until I went into the sanctuary of God; then understood I their end" (Psalm 73:16–17). Thinking about the seeming unfairness of the world was too overwhelming to bear. But then the psalmist walked into the temple and caught a vision of God. When he saw the glory of God, the beauty of living a holy life, the wonder of eternity, he was reassured. He understood that there will come a day when all things are revealed and the scales of justice are balanced. Just a glimpse of God's character is enough to settle the heart, calm the nerves, and inspire patience through suffering.

Rather than asking, "Why is God doing this to me?" a question laced with accusation, try a humbler approach. Ask, "What is God teaching me through this experience?" or, "What can I learn about God, myself, or the world from my situation?" When you take your focus away from yourself and direct it toward God, you will gain both wisdom and peace. God is great and God is good. Both things are still true, even though they don't always seem so. When you adjust your focus and reframe your question, you'll begin to see that.

2. WHAT CAN I BECOME?

After the loss of his family, fortune, and health, Job regretted being alive. While he did not go so far as to contemplate suicide, he clearly saw no point in living. Suffering can bring us to a place of despair. You may feel that despair yourself and voice it through questions like "What's the point of living?"

If you feel so despondent that you have thoughts of harming yourself, put this book down now and call a friend, a physician, or a suicide hotline. Do not stay in this place of despair. Seek help right away. Beyond that, if you are wondering whether your life has any purpose because of the adversity you've faced, you're not alone, but there is a solution. To point us toward a better question, let's consider the example of a great leader who suffered a painful and humiliating failure, King David.

You may know the story of David's affair with Bathsheba, which is recounted in 2 Samuel chapters 11 and 12. The short version is that David committed adultery with Bathsheba, the wife of an officer in David's army. Bathsheba became pregnant, so to cover his tracks David arranged for her husband to be killed in battle. Then David married Bathsheba. Later, the prophet Nathan confronted David with his egregious sin. The consequence? David's own son, the child whom Bathsheba had borne, would die. David was mortified. He was deeply ashamed of his actions and deeply grieved over the loss of his son. In a life with more than its share of adversity, this was by far the lowest moment David had yet experienced. Two people were dead and a family destroyed because of his misdeeds. It would have been easy for David to slip into despair.

Yet David refused to lose heart. He called out to God for forgiveness, and he renewed his pledge to serve the Lord wholeheartedly. Here is a portion of David's great prayer for forgiveness:

> *Have mercy on me, O God,*
> *according to your unfailing love;*
> *according to your great compassion*

blot out my transgressions.
Wash away all my iniquity
and cleanse me from my sin.
For I know my transgressions,
and my sin is always before me. . . .
Surely I was sinful at birth,
sinful from the time my mother conceived me.
Yet you desired faithfulness even in the womb;
you taught me wisdom in that secret place.
Cleanse me with hyssop, and I will be clean;
wash me, and I will be whiter than snow.
Let me hear joy and gladness;
let the bones you have crushed rejoice. . . .
Create in me a pure heart, O God,
and renew a steadfast spirit within me. . . .
Then I will teach transgressors your ways,
so that sinners will turn back to you.
–(Psalm 51:1–3, 5–6, 7–8, 13, NIV)

David did three important things in this prayer. First, he owned the problem. He recognized his sin and confessed it. That's vital. We often blame God, our employer, the bank, or even our family members when our problems are our own doing. If you have failed—either failed in your duty to God or simply made mistakes that have led to some difficulty—don't blame God or others. If you have sinned, confess it and receive God's forgiveness. If you have made mistakes, admit them to yourself and others. If you created the problem, own up to it.

Second, David envisioned grace. He asked God's forgiveness, and he believed that it would be granted. David didn't allow himself to wallow in the past. He knew he was a sinner, conceived in sin, as he put it. But rather than simply regretting the past, David asked for help ("cleanse me"). Don't be afraid to ask God's forgiveness, regardless of what you have done. Likely your sin is not worse than adultery combined with murder. But even if it is, God is eager to forgive any who come to him with a truly contrite heart. Seek grace and you will find it.

Third, David imagined a better future. He said, "Then I will teach sinners your ways," envisioning a time when he would use his own experience of sin and forgiveness to warn and encourage others. David didn't ask, "What's the point of living?" His question was more like, "What can I become?" or, "What can God accomplish in me and through me?" David did not give in to despair; he held on to a sense of purpose.

No matter what your current circumstances may be, God has a plan for your life that includes serving him and serving others. That may be hard to imagine when you're lying in a hospital bed or walking out of bankruptcy court. But don't allow your suffering or your failures to bring despair. Ask, "Lord, what's possible for me now? How can I serve you, even through this experience?" The answer may surprise you. God is a God of second chances. Your life has tremendous value to him.

3. HOW CAN I GLORIFY GOD?

Adversity always makes your life seem smaller. When you lose a job, you lose income and possibility. When you are ill, you lose freedom. Loss accompanies any form of suffering, and that is frustrating. Beyond the loss itself is the sense of frustration at lost possibilities. "Is this all there is for me?" you may wonder. "Are my best days behind me?"

Few people endured more hardship than did the apostle Paul. He was falsely accused and imprisoned, shipwrecked, viciously attacked and left for dead, whipped, and beaten with sticks. Perhaps even more painful than the physical suffering was the opposition he received in his work, often from other Christians. At the close of the book of Acts, Paul had been in prison for two years with no end in sight. Without doubt, that imprisonment narrowed his possibilities. His world had become a lot smaller, and Paul may have been tempted to ask, "So is that it? Are my best days behind me?" But he didn't. Paul wrote, "For I reckon that the sufferings of this present time are not worthy to be compared with the glory which shall be revealed in us" (Romans 8:18). Paul understood what suffering was and he didn't minimize it. Yet he was able to look beyond the effect of adversity on him personally and see the ways that God could be glorified.

Paul also wrote from prison, "Now I want you to know, brothers and sisters, that what has happened to me has actually served to advance the gospel. As a result, it has become clear throughout the whole palace guard and to everyone else that I am in chains for Christ. And because of my chains, most of the brothers and sisters have become confident in the Lord" (Philippians 1:12–14 NIV). Imagine that! Paul was unconcerned about his loss of freedom. He cared only about the advance of the gospel. If his imprisonment helped others, he was glad for it.

When you are tempted to lament the losses in your life, look beyond them to see God's glory. Ask, "How can God be glorified in what I am going through?" Your patience during adversity may be an example to others. Your strong faith, displayed despite your suffering, may inspire others to trust God. Your willingness to forgive and your refusal to exact revenge may bring peace to a family, a workplace, or a community. God can use everything—even what seems like negatives in your life—to advance the good news. Give glory to him in all things.

4. HOW CAN I BLESS OTHERS?

There may be seasons in your life when it seems like *everything* goes wrong. You may handle a simple problem with no trouble, but when the car breaks down, the refrigerator quits, you get fired, and your dog dies all on the same day, you start to wonder, "What's wrong with me?" The more serious your problems are, the more you may wonder why they are happening. In your search for answers, you may land on Job's question, "What did I do to deserve this?"

While that question is understandable, let's pause to look at the assumption that underlies it: *It's all about me!* When we ask, "Why me?" we're assuming that we are at the center of everything that happens in our lives. If it rains, it's raining on *us.* Why? If the economy slows down, it ruins *our* home value. Why would God do that? If we are one of the millions of people who become ill each day, we assume we've been singled out for some reason. Do you see how silly that seems?

Rather than putting yourself at the center of your own troubles, put other people there. That's what Paul seemed to suggest when he wrote, "Blessed be God, even the Father of our Lord Jesus Christ, the Father of mercies, and the God of all comfort; Who comforteth us in all our tribulation, that we may be able to comfort them which are in any trouble, by the comfort wherewith we ourselves are comforted of God" (2 Corinthians 1:3–4). Is it possible that the reason you are facing difficulties has nothing to do with you? Could it be that God has placed you where you are so that you will have the wisdom, experience, compassion, and insight to help someone else? Paul certainly seemed to think so.

When you have been through grief, you know what a grieving person feels. You can offer comfort that would seem shallow coming from others. When you are hospitalized, you are in the one place in town filled with sick people. You have a unique opportunity to display grace and faith to those in need. When you have suffered stress, heartbreak, abuse, or loss, you have a platform from which to reach out to those in need. Rather than asking, "Why did this happen to me?" ask, "How can I bless others through this circumstance?"

5. HOW CAN THIS EXPERIENCE STRENGTHEN MY FAITH?

The first question we encounter in Job's story may be the most profound and asked with the most urgency when you face adversity: "What good is God?" This is the question behind the query from Job's wife, "Are you still maintaining your integrity? Curse God and die!" (Job 2:9 NIV). Adversity can make us question our faith, and it can cause some to abandon it.

As Job discovered, accusing God of being unjust is prideful and misguided. If God really is the one omnipotent, omniscient being in the universe, creator of all that exists, then by what knowledge or authority can we question his judgment? Clearly, if God is God and not some projection of our own sense of justice, then his wisdom and actions are beyond our review. An infant child has no basis to question the decision of a parent, and we have no ability to question God. So let's take the focus off our questioning of God's character and put it on our own. When you suffer, ask, "How can this experience strengthen my faith?" or, "How can I learn to trust God more through what's happening to me?"

We've noted that the apostle Paul suffered a serious problem that he referred to as a "thorn in the flesh" (2 Corinthians 12:7; see Chapter 8). Whatever this thorn was, it caused Paul hardship and was a kind of weakness. Yet even in this unwelcome problem, Paul saw a benefit in that it strengthened his character and his faith. First, he said that it was given "lest [he] should be exalted above measure through the abundance of revelations..." (verse 7). Paul saw himself as privileged because of a vision he'd been given, and he saw this "thorn" as a way of keeping him humble. It helped him grow spiritually. He also wrote, "Most gladly therefore will I rather glory in my infirmities, that the power of Christ may rest upon me. Therefore I take pleasure in infirmities, in reproaches, in necessities, in persecutions, in distresses for Christ's sake: for when I am weak, then am I strong" (2 Corinthians 12:9–10). Paul realized that the occasions when he felt the most confined, inadequate, weak, or helpless were the very times God could more fully display his power through the apostle. Paul's weakness revealed God's strength.

Adversity, regardless of its source, is a tool God can use to deepen your faith and strengthen your commitment to him. It's also one of the best ways for him to get your attention. As C. S. Lewis observed, "God whispers to us in our pleasures, speaks in our conscience, but shouts in our pains: it is His megaphone to rouse a deaf world."[32] When you feel pain—or the discomfort

---

32. C. S. Lewis, *The Problem of Pain* (San Francisco: HarperOne, 1996), 91.

that comes from any form of adversity—ask, "Lord, how do you want to use this experience to strengthen my faith?"

When you focus doubt and suspicion on God by asking, "Why did you do this to me?" you will remain stuck right where you are. But when you turn your appraising eye toward yourself, you'll see the gaps in your character, the weaknesses in your spirit, and the opportunities to deepen your faith. Like Paul, you will come to thank God even for the hard times in your life because those are the times that lead you closer to the Father.

GOD WILL, YOU CAN

Before we leave this subject of learning through hard times, let's be sure to affirm that God is gentle and caring toward those who suffer, and there is hope in every situation. God is still in control, and he can do anything. I have learned that the sun has a sinking spell every night, but it comes back up every morning. You may experience the darkest hour of your life, but that hour will be only sixty minutes long. And it really is true that the harder you fall, the higher you bounce. God is doing a work in you to mature you and help you grow so that you can reach greater heights than ever before. He will comfort you, teach you, keep you, advance you through this adversity. Trust him, as Job did. Whatever your situation, worship the Father.

Difficult times, trials, suffering, frustrations—they all bring to mind a single question: "Why?" That question is layered with many more questions about God, the nature of the world, and your future prospects in life. Often, we keep ourselves stuck in place by asking the wrong questions—questions that put us, our hurts, and our wants at the center.

Maybe it's time for you to ask a better question, a question that focuses on God and his kingdom, a question that puts others, rather than yourself, in first place. We cannot control the tragic things that happen to us, but we can control the way we face up to them. When you come to the Lord asking, "Father, what good can you do in me and through me today?" you will find grace, healing, wisdom, and growth. You will learn from what you suffer, and you will overcome.

THE SUCCESSFUL SEVEN

- List the questions you have about your current situation, then circle those that seem to come from a place of hope and draw a line through those motivated by doubt.

- Name the main thing that you have learned from your current suffering, then share that learning with someone.

- Name three people who have been through circumstances like the one you're facing. Ask one of them to share his or her life lessons with you.

- Pray, asking, "Lord, how can I grow through what I am experiencing?" and write down the answer you receive.

- Identify someone who faces a problem similar to yours and offer encouragement.

- Write down three things you hope God will make possible for you and share your list with a friend.

- Memorize Proverbs 4:7.

◇

12
Faith for What's Left

The thief cometh not, but for to steal, and to kill,
and to destroy: I am come that they might have life,
and that they might have it more abundantly.
—John 10:10

THE WINNING ATTITUDE

There are better days ahead.

FUTURE VISION

Adversity has stolen a lot from Jill Viles. This Iowa wife and mom suffers from not one but two rare genetic disorders, Emery-Dreifuss muscular dystrophy, which primarily affects muscles in the arms and legs as well as the heart muscle, and partial lipodystrophy, a genetic mutation that causes a loss of fat in the limbs, leaving veins and muscles to stand out. The result is that Jill's arms and legs are pencil thin and very weak. These diseases have robbed her of her ability to walk and much of her independence.

Because of their onset early in life, they also robbed Jill of the childhood many children enjoy. She endured taunts from other kids about her appearance, especially her thin and veiny legs. While many children were growing stronger and enjoying sports, Jill was growing weaker and more frail. She would fall often. To make matters worse, her condition stumped experts in nearly every field of medicine. Throughout her teen years, Jill received no diagnosis and therefore had no idea what was causing her condition—or how to treat it. She said, "I didn't know things about life expectancy, or even to explain to another person, 'Okay, this is what I have and why.' You just really have a sense that you can't go on with your life if you don't have these basic questions answered." Illness had stolen her childhood, and it seemed to be stealing her future as well.

What the disease could not steal was Jill's optimism, determination, or hope. When doctors were unable to diagnose her condition, Jill set out to research it for herself. At age nineteen, Jill determined that she had Emery-Dreifuss, but doctors refused to believe her. So Jill sent samples of her blood to a DNA lab in Italy to confirm the diagnosis. The results not only gave Jill certainty about her condition but also saved her father's life. Realizing that he too was affected by the disease, she urged him to seek medical treatment. Doctors discovered that his heart was barely functioning and immediately inserted a pacemaker.

During the mid-1990s, while working as an intern at a research lab, Jill's reading led her to suspect that she had a second malady, partial lipodystrophy. Again, doctors politely dismissed her ideas. Jill dropped her inquiry and concentrated on beginning a family. Yet her disease continued to weaken her, eventually confining her to a motorized scooter.

Fast forward to 2013. Then age thirty-nine, Jill saw online photos of Canadian sprinter Priscilla Lopes-Schliep. This Olympic medalist had unusually strong limbs with bulging muscles, making her appear the polar opposite of Jill, whose emaciated arms and legs looked more like toothpicks. But Jill saw a connection. In Priscilla's lean, muscular physique, Jill detected signs of the same malady she knew she possessed but which no one else could see—partial lipodystrophy. After making contact with the sprinter, both women were tested for this rare genetic disorder, and sure enough, both possessed a form of it. Neither woman's body could properly retain fat. For the third time, Jill Viles, despite the many limitations she faced, had seen what no one else could.

There's more.

When the test results came in, Priscilla had been on her way to lunch, preparing to order a big juicy hamburger and fries. Her doctor called at that moment and warned her to eat nothing more than salad, saying she was on track for a pancreatitis attack. Despite her physical fitness, the undetected lipodystrophy had left Priscilla with fifteen times the normal amount of fat in her blood. The next burger could have landed her in the emergency room. Jill Viles' vision and persistence had, once again, saved a life.[33]

One of the keys to overcoming adversity in your life is to adopt the outlook displayed by this determined Midwestern mom. You must focus not on what you've lost but on what remains. Do not

---

33. David Epstein, "The DIY Scientist, the Olympian, and the Mutated Gene: How a woman whose muscles disappeared discovered she shared a disease with a muscle-bound Olympic medalist," *ProPublica* website, January 15, 2016, https://www.propublica.org/article/muscular-dystrophy-patient-olympic-medalist-same-genetic-mutation. The quote from Jill Viles is taken from the video bearing the same title and found on the same page as the article.

become mired in the past but look at the future. The hardship you face may rob you of money, health, opportunity, or comfort, but you don't have to let it steal your soul. It's fine to grieve for what's lost but keep faith for what's left.

The biblical hero who illustrates this principle is an unnamed woman in the Old Testament who also had lost a great deal. Her husband had died, and she was on the verge of losing everything to his creditors. Her dramatic story illustrates the power of faith in preserving the resources you have left and leveraging them to move into the future. It will inspire you to keep your eyes focused on God's possibilities for your life.

DON'T PANIC

The story of this widow is recorded in 2 Kings 4:1–7. It begins when the woman, whose husband had been one of the prophets, sought out the great prophet Elisha for help. The woman's husband had died and left her with a large debt. She told Elisha, "Thy servant my husband is dead; and thou knowest that thy servant did fear the LORD: and the creditor is come to take unto him my two sons to be bondmen" (2 Kings 4:1). She had lost her husband and was about to lose her sons as well. She must have been at her wit's end but this widow didn't panic. She calmly went to Elisha seeking help.

If you have ever had problems with debt, you may have an inkling of what this woman was facing. Though creditors today can do nothing so drastic as seizing one's children, they can sometimes confiscate property and garnish wages. The fear of loss can be overwhelming. A similar fear may grip your mind when you face adversity of other kinds. You see what you have lost and what you have the potential to lose, and that causes anxiety. When you have a health problem, you lose strength and ability. You may also fear the loss of income, the loss of your job or home, or further losses to your health. What if the illness gets worse? When you have a financial problem, fear spreads its tentacles into other areas of your life as well. The stress from financial strain can affect your health, your marriage, or your work. Worry about paying bills, anxiety about losing your home, stress over dealing with creditors—it can be exhausting.

In a state of fear and confusion, it's possible to make a bad situation worse. For example, the fear of losing your home may lead you to borrow even more money, compounding your problems with debt. The fear of losing a relationship may cause you to do something foolish or irrational, further complicating the situation. At these times, the devil is always present to suggest selfish, devious, or just plain foolish ways to deal with your problems. You may compound your misery by making one bad choice after another.

When you feel afraid about the future, remember this: The devil is a thief and a liar. Satan will take from you all that he can. Never trust him. Hold on to your faith; hold on to hope.

There are a number of biblical names for our adversary, and they reveal his character. He is called the devil, the father of lies (John 8:44), and Beelzebub, meaning lord of the flies (1 Kings 1:2; Matthew 12:24), Belial, meaning worthless (2 Corinthians 6:15), Apollyon, meaning destroyer (Revelation 9:11), and Satan, the accuser of the brethren (Revelation 12:10). Jesus pointed to one particular aspect of the devil's character, calling him a thief. In the same breath, however, Jesus pointed out that he, Jesus, is the giver of abundant life: "The thief cometh not, but for to steal, and to kill, and to destroy: I am come that they might have life, and that they might have it more abundantly" (John 10:10). The common theme is that the devil wants to steal or destroy everything—including you. But Jesus is the giver of life. That leads us to two important lessons that will keep you from getting panicked in the face of adversity.

First, don't be surprised that you encounter problems or experience loss of various kinds. The devil is a powerful force to be reckoned with and for the time being, he has the freedom to wreak havoc in our lives. We face illness, natural disasters, accidents, and all these are the devil's work, the result of sin in the world. Satan also specifically targets us for hardship. We learn this from the story of Job, where Satan is pictured as singling out one man, Job, for the loss of his fortune, his family, and his health (see Job 1–2, and Chapter 11 of this book).

Also, some of the hardship we face may come specifically because of our faith in Christ. We should expect that. The apostle Peter wrote, "Beloved, think it not strange concerning the fiery trial which is to try you, as though some strange thing happened unto you" (1 Peter 4:12). Persecution or opposition based on our faith is normal. If the world despised Jesus, how much more will it despise his followers? The apostle Paul was even more direct: "Yea, and all that will live godly in Christ Jesus shall suffer persecution" (2 Timothy 3:12).

Suffering is normal in that it is something we all go through. Bad things happen. Satan oppresses people, especially God's elect. Christians face hardship and even persecution for their faith. We do have an enemy in this world, and he is active. We should not be surprised when we suffer various forms of hardship, trial, or adversity.

A second important truth is that we don't have to give in to fear. The devil is a liar, and he schemes to make our lives worse, not better. His promises are illusions, and his word is no good. Do not fall victim to fear or anxiety because of his schemes. "Be sober, be vigilant; because your adversary the devil, as a roaring lion, walketh about, seeking whom he may devour" (1 Peter 5:8). Be alert for the devil's schemes, and don't let him eat you alive. Instead, "resist the devil, and he will flee from you" (James 4:7).

When you feel anxious about the future and are tempted to do something foolish, stop. Remember that the devil offers you nothing good. Resist him. Pray to the Lord, asking for peace of mind, clear thoughts, and the ability to persevere. The Spirit will not leave you alone. He will help. "There hath no temptation taken you but such as is common to man: but God is faithful, who will not suffer you to be tempted above that ye are able; but will with the temptation also make a way to escape, that ye may be able to bear it" (1 Corinthians 10:13). Remember that in the same breath that Jesus called the devil a thief, he pointed to himself as the giver of life. Don't be panicked by the problems you face. When you feel most anxious about your circumstances, trust Jesus.

KEEP YOUR FAITH

The widow in our story had already lost her husband, and then the creditors came for what was most precious to her—her children. That's where she made her stand, reaching out to Elisha for help. This woman refused to accept the idea that she would lose *everything*. She called upon the great prophet because that was her best way to call on God. Remember that Jesus had not yet come. He had not yet taught us how to pray by simply calling out to God, our Father. The Holy Spirit had not yet been given. By reaching out to the prophet Elisha, this woman was calling on God. This was a great demonstration of faith.

As with this poor widow, Satan will eventually come after the things that are most important in your life. By that I do not mean money, possessions, or even health. These things are temporary. All material things can be replaced, and we know that our bodies will eventually fail. Our true hope is in heaven. And that's exactly what Satan wants to take from you—your faith in Christ and the joy, peace, and hope that come from it. Satan doesn't want simply to take your money or your health, not even your life. He's after your soul.

Remember that when you are facing adversity of any kind. The trouble itself is not the real issue. It is a spiritual test of your willingness to trust God. James the apostle pointed this out when he wrote, "My brethren, count it all joy when ye fall into divers temptations; Knowing this, that the trying of your faith worketh patience. But let patience have her perfect work, that ye may be perfect and entire, wanting nothing" (James 1:2–4). We get upset when we face adversity because all we can see is the inconvenience, loss, or pain that it represents. Look deeper. Each trial is a test of your faith, and that faith will grow stronger as you become more and more mature through adversity.

As we saw in the last chapter, Job suffered the loss of every material thing in life, including his health. But he had one thing left: his faith. His statement of confidence in God is one of the most moving in Scripture: "Though he slay me, yet will I trust in him" (Job 13:15). Satan took everything from Job it is possible to take, but he could not touch Job's heart. The same is true for you.

Jesus Christ is the giver of life, and his power is unlimited. We who are in Christ have a guaranteed victory; Jesus sealed that victory by rising from the grave. The godly widow called out to Elisha, who is a type or representative of Christ in the Old Testament. You can call on Jesus too. Ask for his help. Open your heart to his Spirit. You cannot fail because he cannot fail. If you find yourself lost for words, pray the prayer of David recorded in Psalm 5 (TLB):

> O Lord, hear me praying; listen to my plea, O God my King, for I will never pray to anyone but you. Each morning I will look to you in heaven and lay my requests before you, praying earnestly.
>
> I know you get no pleasure from wickedness and cannot tolerate the slightest sin. Therefore, proud sinners will not survive your searching gaze, for how you hate their evil deeds. You will destroy them for their lies; how you abhor all murder and deception.
>
> But as for me, I will come into your Temple protected by your mercy and your love; I will worship you with deepest awe.
>
> Lord, lead me as you promised me you would; otherwise my enemies will conquer me. Tell me clearly what to do, which way to turn. For they cannot speak one truthful word. Their hearts are filled to the brim with wickedness. Their suggestions are full of the stench of sin and death. Their tongues are filled with flatteries to gain their wicked ends. O God, hold them responsible. Catch them in their

own traps; let them fall beneath the weight of their own transgressions, for they rebel against you.

But make everyone rejoice who puts his trust in you. Keep them shouting for joy because you are defending them. Fill all who love you with your happiness. For you bless the godly man, O Lord; you protect him with your shield of love.

You have a shield of faith and God has a shield of love. When you lift your shield, he lifts his. No scheme of the devil can penetrate that armor. The devil is a dream stealer, a life taker, and a relationship robber, but he can't take what is most precious unless you let him. Satan cannot take your obedience; only you can choose to turn way from God. Satan cannot steal your joy; only you can surrender your happiness. Satan cannot take your peace of mind; only you can give in to worry. Satan cannot take your faith; only you can give it away. Hold on to your joy. Hold on to your hope. Hold on to your faith. Satan can wreak havoc on every area of your life, but he cannot touch your soul. Keep the faith.

FOCUS ON WHAT REMAINS

When the widow in our story asked Elisha for help, he asked two simple questions in return: "And Elisha said unto her, What shall I do for thee? tell me, what hast thou in the house?" (2 Kings 4:2). His first question, "What shall I do for thee?" seems to indicate that Elisha himself was also poor. Prophets had no income, after all, depending on donations. He did not have the resources to pay off her debt so Elisha directed her back to her own situation, asking about what resources she had. Obviously, there was little there—otherwise the woman would have sold it herself and paid off the debt. If she had been sitting on a pot of gold, she wouldn't have come to Elisha in the first place. But Elisha challenged her to look deeper. What resources *did* she possess? What did she have to work with?

That's a question we often overlook. When facing adversity, we focus so much on what's been lost that we fail to see what remains. We focus on the money we lost and forget about the funds remaining. We become obsessed with the love that slipped away and fail to see those who continue to love us. We think more about the person who has passed away than about those who remain in our lives. We don't see the potential in money, strength, or opportunity we have left because it seems like nothing compared to what we had—and what we need.

You can observe that attitude in the widow's response to Elisha. She said, "Thine handmaid hath not any thing in the house, save a pot of oil" (verse 2). Did you catch that? Elisha asked what she had in the house and she said, "Nothing. Well, nothing but a pot of oil." That's typical thinking for most people who have suffered a loss. They can't see what remains. In answer to the question, "What do you have left?" they are likely to say—

- "Nothing. Well, nothing but a few dollars in the bank."
- "Nothing. Well, nothing but my health."
- "Nothing. Well, nothing but my spouse and children."
- "Nothing. Well, nothing but my business connections."
- "Nothing. Well, nothing but my home."
- "Nothing. Well, nothing but my church family."

They become so focused on the loss and so overwhelmed by their need that they cannot see the value of the resources that remain. But God can.

God's power when added to anything makes it more than abundant. Our problem is not that we have few resources; it's that we have little faith. Once when the disciples asked Jesus why their prayers had been ineffective, he said, "Because of your unbelief: for verily I say unto you, If ye have faith as a grain of mustard seed, ye shall say unto this mountain, Remove hence to yonder place; and it shall remove; and nothing shall be impossible unto you" (Matthew 17:20). Your tiny resource plus God's power equals great possibility. Jesus demonstrated that when the disciples were panicked over how to feed five thousand people. When they complained about the problem, Jesus asked a question remarkably similar to the one Elisha asked the widow: "How many loaves have ye?" (Mark 6:38). In other words, "What do you have?" Don't look at the need, Jesus was saying. Look at the resource. Jesus took the tiny offering, looked up to heaven and blessed it, then handed out more than enough food to feed the entire crowd (Mark 6:41–43).

God spoke the world into existence *from nothing.* Imagine what he can do with the little bit you have. When a blind man came to Jesus for healing, he spat on the ground, made mud with the saliva, and put it on the man's eyes, healing him. If Jesus can make a mud ball into an eyeball, he can certainly do something positive with your last twenty dollars, your one remaining friend, or the lone job opportunity open to you. Focus on what remains. The widow in this story took a long minute to remember that she did, in fact, have some resources to work with—or rather, for God to work with. Stop. Think. What resources remain in your life or in your situation? What can you offer to God that he can use for his glory?

TAKE ACTION

If you've listened to much country music, you know that many of the songs are about loss. The singer often tells a sad story about losing a marriage, or a job, or a dog—or all three. Someone has suggested that if you play country music backwards, the wife comes back, the job comes back, and the dog comes home. I don't know if that's true, but the end of our story about the widow is a bit like playing the song backwards. A story of loss and heartache somehow turned into a story of abundance. That happened because the widow was willing to take a bold action.

Hearing that the widow had one pot of oil left in the house, Elisha gave her this instruction: "Go, borrow thee vessels abroad of all thy neighbours, even empty vessels; borrow not a few. And when thou art come in, thou shalt shut the door upon thee and upon thy sons, and shalt pour out into all those vessels, and thou shalt set aside that which is full" (2 Kings 4:3–4). That sounds crazy. I can almost imagine what the woman must have thought: *Didn't you hear me? I said I have only a little oil. I can't fill up one of my neighbor's jars, let alone many.* The instruction didn't make sense. It was like God telling Jeremiah to invest in real estate shortly before all property would be confiscated by the enemy (see Jeremiah 32:6–13). It was like Jesus telling the disciples to have five thousand people sit down in rows, expecting a meal, when they had only five loaves and two fish to distribute (Mark 6:39). Instructions like this don't make sense in the "real world," we think. But when you have the faith to see what God can do with just a small resource, it makes perfect sense.

The woman did exactly as Elisha had instructed. She borrowed the pots, went home, and closed the door. That last step was important because she certainly would have faced ridicule if her neighbors had realized what she was doing. You, too, will face critics and scoffers when you act in faith. You may be able to focus on the resources that remain and offer them to God, but others may see that as folly. They won't believe that a person who has failed in marriage can finally find love. They'll have a hard time understanding why someone would change careers to follow a calling. They may not accept the idea that a person with a disability can be productive and successful in a career. To move beyond your loss, you'll have to shut out negative voices and listen to the Lord.

The result of the widow's bold action was a miracle of multiplication. She and her sons formed a kind of bucket brigade, with them bringing the empty jars into the house and taking out the full ones. The woman stayed inside, filling one jug after another from that single jar of oil. Before long, they had filled every vessel in the neighborhood, and the original jar remained full. The woman was able to sell the oil, pay off the debt, and save her family. And when she told Elisha about it, he said, "You and your sons can live on what is left" (2 Kings 4:7 NIV).

This woman hadn't been pouring oil so much as pouring out her faith in obedience to God. She was willing to trust the Word delivered through the prophet and to take bold action. She put feet to her faith, and God responded. He'll do the same for you when you take action based on his Word.

What's left of your life? Satan may have taken a bite out of it, or perhaps he's devoured nearly everything. Have faith for what remains. Love with what's left of your heart. Work with what's left of your energy. Live with what's left of your health. Plan with what's left of your dream. Serve with what's left of your passion. God will meet you in that faithful action, and he'll bless what little you have. When you've got nothing left but God, you have enough to start again.

LIVE ON WHAT'S LEFT

The enemy wants to destroy your life, but he cannot steal your faith. Jesus wants to give you an abundant life, and he will respond to your faith. That's a winning combination. From an overcomer's perspective, the story of the widow is about refusing to quit. It's about holding on to hope and acting in faith, no matter how bad things may seem. There are possibilities in your life, if you have eyes to see them. Don't listen to the thief. Don't wallow in the past by focusing on what you've lost. And don't be surprised by hardship. You will face losses in life. Hard times will come. Focus on the future. See the possibilities. Keep the faith when things look hopeless. The devil may have taken much, but he cannot take your faith. You have more than enough to live on what remains.

THE SUCCESSFUL SEVEN

- Take inventory of your life, listing the resources and opportunities available to you.

- Pray, asking God, "What would you have me do with the resources you've given me?"

- Consult a friend or mentor to discuss your plans for the future.

- List the fears you have about the future and the temptations that spring from them, then ask a friend to pray specifically about those fears.

- Identify the critics who discourage your dreams and determine how you will minimize or counteract those voices.

- Choose a bold, faithful action that you can take this week, then do it.

- Memorize John 10:10.

◇

AFTERWORD
I Refuse to Lose

Jim Paul had an amazing career. From humble beginnings
in a small Kentucky town, he gained a fortune in com-
modities trading. He was even appointed to the board of governors of the Chicago Mercantile Exchange, the largest futures and
options trading site in the world. In his book, *What I Learned
Losing a Million Dollars*, Paul describes the thrill of winning, including the time he made $248,000 in a single day of trading. But
as the book's title implies, the story didn't end there. In the span
of a single year, Jim Paul lost all of his money, went $400,000 in
debt, lost his membership in the exchange, his job, and his seat
on the board of governors.[5] During one particularly bad stretch,
he lost between $20,000 and $25,000 *per day* for weeks on end,
always believing that the next day's trading would pull him out of
the hole. He was losing a fortune and couldn't see it. Worse, he
couldn't quit. A senior manager at his brokerage firm finally had
to pull the plug on his trading.

Incredibly, Paul was undeterred. "I wasn't going to quit playing," he wrote, "but I was going to quit losing."[6] After going broke,
Paul examined his experience and learned something profound

---

5. Jim Paul and Brendan Moynihan, *What I Learned Losing a Million Dollars*, (New York: Columbia University Press, 2013), 74.
6. Ibid., 2.

about winning and losing, particularly as it applies to making money in the markets. There are lots of ways to win based on a fact-based analysis of the market, he determined. But there are only a few ways to lose. And all of them have to do with psychological factors that keep a person locked into a losing position.[7] To put it another way, winning is based on knowledge, but losing is a mindset.

The same is true of your desire to win in the spiritual life. If you are to overcome the adversity you now face and emerge as a stronger, more vibrant, and fully blessed Christian, you must recognize that winning results from a knowledge of the truth while losing comes from flawed thinking. Winning is a revelation; losing is a mindset. You can choose to win by gaining a fresh revelation from God and applying that truth to your life. By the same token, you choose to lose by clinging to the same losing attitudes that have left you stuck for so long.

What are some characteristics of the losing mindset? We've mentioned many of them in this book. Here's a review of the most deadly.

Willful Blindness. You choose to lose when you refuse to accept the reality of your situation, pretending that you have no problems or have no responsibility for solving them.

Learned Helplessness. You choose to lose when you accept the idea that you are helpless and can do nothing to affect your situation.

Timidity. You choose to lose when you are unwilling to trust God and take action because it seems risky.

Arrogance. You choose to lose when you won't admit that you need help, believing that willpower alone can solve your problems.

---

7. Ibid., xviii, 3.

Ignorance. You choose to lose when you refuse to learn from your mistakes.

Negativity. You choose to lose when you harbor negative thoughts, reacting based on suspicion and fear.

Self-Doubt. You choose to lose when you see yourself as a loser rather than as an overcomer, as God has declared you to be.

Poor Associations. You choose to lose when you surround yourself with temptation, laziness, and doubt.

Lack of Purpose. You choose to lose when you won't look beyond your immediate circumstances to embrace your calling.

Selfishness. You choose to lose when you think the world revolves around you, rather than seeing yourself as a servant of others.

Suspicion. You choose to lose when you see every setback in your life as a reason to accuse or mistrust God, rather than as an opportunity to glorify him.

Despair. You choose to lose when you wallow in the past rather than seeing possibilities for the future.

The devil, your adversary, would like nothing more than for you to remain stuck in a losing mindset. So long as you think of yourself as helpless, powerless, victimized, and ineffective, you will be. A losing mindset will cause you to lose every time.

But God has declared you to be a winner. We who believe in Christ are "more than conquerors though him that loved us" (Romans 8:37). Though the thief has taken much from us, Jesus Christ has come to give us an abundant life (John 10:10). When you accept this revelation from the Word, adopt your new identity as a victorious child of God, and apply biblical truth to your life, you have a strategy for moving forward. You will overcome.

My great hope and prayer for you is that you will put the principles and attitudes outlined in this book into immediate action. I pray that you will refuse to lose and will accept the victory that God has for you.

Choose to believe that change is possible. Choose to trust God, to develop a relationship with him, and to obey him.

Understand that God has a bright future in store for you. Know that you can begin claiming that blessing now. Realize that you must put yourself in position to win by seeking out positive, faithful people and avoiding those who inspire doubt and fear. Grasp the truth that God will use even your failure and weakness for his glory.

Believe that your life has a purpose. Become a person who invests in others. Become a student of growth, learning even from your suffering. And never stop believing that there are better days ahead.

When you make these choices, apply these principles, and adopt these attitudes, you will overcome the adversity in your life. God's power can be and will be displayed in your life. You will win. We know that the consequences of sin—our own sins, the sins of others, and the sinfulness of the world—may not be fully erased during our lifetime. Overcoming adversity does not mean that you will never suffer, never feel pain, or never face problems. As long as you live, you will deal with the brokenness of the world and be subject to its effects. But you can overcome. You can have hope. You can have joy. You can have purpose. You can grow. You can succeed. By God's grace, you can be a different person tomorrow than you were yesterday.

Winning is a revelation; losing is a mindset. You now have the revelation—the truth from God's Word—that will enable you to overcome. It's time to leave the losing mindset behind. Choose to win. Refuse to lose. By God's grace, you will overcome!

◇